My Autobiography

BY

John Harris

MY AUTOBIOGRAPHY.

BY

JOHN HARRIS.

WITH A PHOTOGRAPHIC PORTRAIT OF THE AUTHOR.

LONDON:
Hamilton, Adams, and Co.

Falmouth: The Author.   Penryn: John Gill and Son.
Exeter: F. Clapp, Roseneath, St. James's Road.

1882.

PREFACE.

The author has been solicited by several of his friends to publish his Autobiography in a seperate form, which first appeared, in connexion with his "Two Giants," in 1878. In compliance with their request he brings out this little book, enlarging the original sketch, and adding considerably thereto. He trusts his lifelong perseverance under difficulties, his untiring struggles after literature, and his unflagging pursuit of song under all circumstances, may induce not a few of the young of his own country to pursue with indomitable zeal the pleasant path of right. To them, as well as to his intelligent countrymen generally, he trustfully commits the following imperfect pages, with the hope of the scattered grain bearing some little fruit after many days.

The woodcuts, as well as the author's photographic portrait, have been produced by his invalid son; and the few poems at the end of the book are now published for the first time.

FALMOUTH,
NOVEMBER, 1882.

CONTENTS.

MY AUTOBIOGRAPHY.

CHAPTER I.

EARLY LIFE.

James Hogg. About Myself. The Eldest Child. "Six Chimneys." When Born. Granite Porch. Uncle Matthew. Bag of Gunpowder. Names of my Parents. Grandmother Smith. Parish Feast. Fireside Tales. Dante's "Inferno." Christmas Eve. Anxious Watchers. Santa Claus. Singular Story. Granite Stile. Fervent Petition. Angel's Visit. My Father a Tributer. Farm on the Hill. One Book. Force of Gentleness. Autumn Walk. Sweet Love-lesson. Merited Chastisement. Gwithian Sands. The Great Sea. Aunt Margery. Old Deal Form. Redeemed from the Wild. Moonlight Fays. Early Inspiration. Grandfather Ben. Shakespere and Milton. Witty Saying. No trace of Ancestry. Loss of the Farm. Widow's Struggle. Lack of Books. Grandmother Joan. Crisp Cake. Mountain Goats. Elder-tree. Bent Beggar. Lantern Ring. Lost Child. Rick of Turf. Alarum Clock. Flint and Steel. Hangman Barrow. Crock of Guineas. Unfortunate Horseman. My Mother's Teaching. Led to Chapel. Trout-fishing. Heavy Burden. Evening Visitant. The Mountain. Nature's Lessons. Annual Gathering. Busy Workers. George the Bachelor. The Old Hall. Festive Jingles. Freak of my Uncle. Sunday School. Holy Sensation. Dark District. Sabbath Employment. The Six Hawthorns. .... Page 1.

CHAPTER II.

DOWN IN THE MINE.

Village Schoolmistress. "Robinson Crusoe." First Book. "Cottar's Saturday Night," Fireside Reading. Love of Song. "Pilgrim's Progress." Summer Storm. Severe Master. Old Squeers. John Roberts. Forest Gate. Over the Moor. Kept In. Poor Pen. Schoolboy Ramble. Among the Flowers. True Devotion. Patient Cobbler. Striving to Rise. First Verses. Place of Study. Novel Ink. Tea-wrappers. Rhyme Reading. Two Pounds of Paint. Saddler Dick. Too Positive. Carnmenellis. Feathery Litchen. Love of Home. Tregonning Hill. Aged Questioner. Leave School. Go to Work. Uncle George. Bob and Fly. Roasted Potatoes. Pig-killing. Old Tin Streamer. Jews'-House. Threepence a Day. The Nine Maidens. Song Seeking. My Bower. Great Change. Going to the Mine. Varied Employment. Repeating my Rhymes. Serious Struggle. Cheering Voices. Under the Surface. Long Ladders. Dangerous Descent. Roped to my Father. Boyish Disappointment. Tedious Climbing. Wheeling the Mineral. Knocking my Joints. Heroic Resolve. Strange Horseman. Bottom Hill. Over the Rubbish. Up the Steep. The Vanishing Echo. Superstition. Cottager's Daughter. Wizard Defeated. Courting the Muse. Copying my Verses. Silent Journey. Poetry everything. Kirke White. Rector's Visit. Purchase a Dictionary. Difficult Words. Improve my Grammar. Ogilvie. Slate and Nail. Stumpy Pencil. Shunning the Crowd. Reedy Barn. Yearning for Solitude. Pursuit of Literature. Fulfilment of Duty. Poetic Education. Turf Cutting. Blistered Hands. Bog Peat. Druid Relics. Great Chamber. Little Leisure. Writing on Plaster. Improving my Time. The Meadow Ditch. Fifing my Verses. Usual Desk. Satirical Pieces. Stupid Dentist. Page 23.

CHAPTER III.

HOME LIFE.

Campbell's "Gertrude." Robert Pollok. Rejected Manuscript. Old Golly. Lesson Learnt. Connor Bar. Wicked Advisers. Grave in the Wilderness. First Printed

Verses. Singing Blind Man. Purchase Three Books. Pacing the Carns. Editor's Encouragement. Shunning the Alehouse. At my Rhyming. Find a Wife. The Two-roomed Dwelling. Tenpence a Day. The Lode Improves. Building a House. In the Quarry. Carrying Stone. Writing on the Cart Shafts. Splitting Granite. Perseverance Rewarded. Long for a Study. Among the Gorse Brakes. "Romeo and Juliet." Great Bliss. "Childe Harold." Love for Burns. Presentation Copy. Heedless Strictures. Dolcoath Mine. Down in the Depths. Rarefied Air. Naked to the Waist. Hung in Ropes. Life on a Nail. Smiting the Drill. Sleeping on Flints. Pangs of Thirst. Song Attendants. Writing on Wedges. Breaking Rocks. Pleasing Acknowledgement. Out in the Rain. No Overcoat. Rocking Baby. Walks with my Children. War Fiend. Great Conflict. Home Attractions. Small Earnings. Pocket of Blackberries. Happy Watchers. Not Poor. Hymn to my Waiting Ones. Recent Effusion. Event at Supper. Child's First Prayer. Weeping Reader. Troon Moor Home. Evening Story. Poem Writing. Doctor Smith. Desire to Publish. Judges' Verdict. My First Book. Kind Reception. The Agent's Interest. Witholding Aid. Not Daunted. Fire of Rhymes. Visit the Land's End. First and Last. Startled Sea Birds. Longing for Release. Thy will be Done. ...... Page 54.

CHAPTER IV.

BOOK MAKING.

Narrow Escapes. Severed Chain. Man Engine Accident. Sudden Explosion. Sunday School Treat. Full of Rocks. Uncle Will. The Extinguished Candle. A Climb in the Dark. The Unguarded Shaft. Into the Light. Mrs. Balfour. First Post Office Order. Word Pictures. Two Young Cornishmen. Preparing a Second Volume. Edward Bastin. Become a Scripture Reader. The Silver Teapot. Land's End. Pleased Reader. Mountain Prophet. Devonshire Poet. Drive to Kynance Cove. Story of Carn Brea. Letter from a Lady. Essay Useful. Shakespere's Shrine. Luda. Battle with the Fates. Self Sacrifices. Shakespere Watch. Well to Try. My Wife's

Message. Successful Competitor. Postman's Exultation. Appropriate Engraving. Bath Abbey. Congratulatory Letters. The Doctor's Claim. Preserved Ode. Shakespere Museum. Out of Cornwall. Sounds at Shottery. Monument of Chatterton. George Muller. England's Wealth. Bulo. London Friends. Cruise of the Cutter. Baroness Burdett Coutts. No Publisher. Peace Pages. Tracts and Essays. Wayside Pictures. Alexander R. Gray. A Guinea a Copy. Royal Literary Fund. Newspaper Articles. Mountain Mat. A Study at Last. Walks with the Wild Flowers. Earl Northbrook. Tales and Poems. Affliction. Reduction of Salary. Loss of my Study. The Two Giants. Monro. Tercentenary Ode. Professor Longfellow. Linto and Laneer. S. C. Hall. Other Pieces. My Son's Woodcuts. Loss in the City. Remittance from London. Publishing Expenses. Royal Bounty Fund. John Bright. Bank Failure. Mr. Gladstone's Grant. Doctor Rogers. Old Account Book. Hymn Useful. Record of my Mother. Object of Writing. Excelsior. Glossary. .... Page 79.

UNPUBLISHED POEMS.

THE DAISY MEADOW	107
MY EARLY HOME	108
THE BRIGHT PATH	109
TEMPTATION RESISTED	110
THE PRAYING MOTHER	111
THE REQUEST	112
THEOBRIGHT	114
DO THE BEST YOU CAN	115
LISTEN	116
LIFE'S EVENING	117
HYMN	118
A BIRTHDAY HYMN	119
TESTIMONIAL VERSES	120
CONRAD AND THE STORK	121
THE MILLER AND HIS NAG	124
LIVING POETICAL WRITERS	125

A COTTAGE mid the moorland reed
    Smiled by the fairies' turning;
And there it was that Davie Drake
    First saw the light of morning.
He had a pleasant loving face;
    His eyes with joy were beaming;
And he among his native flowers
    Appeared like April dreaming.

The seasons ran their annual rounds,
    The sun and stars grew older;
Ambition seized his thoughtful soul,
    And Davie Drake was bolder.
A voice seemed sounding on the hill,
    And whispering through the brier:
"Climb, Davie, climb; the way is free
    To higher things and higher."

His friends were poor, his kindred few;
    His father was a hedger;
His only uncle on the cliff
    A weather-beaten dredger.
He had no one his mind to guide
    To teach him e'en the letters:
So Davie said, "I'll teach myself,
    And climb towards my betters."

The way was long, the hill was high,
    The rough ascent distressing;
But Davie boldly persevered:
    Still step by step progressing.

Hope walked beside him, chanting sweet,
  In rainbow-rich attire:
"Climb, Davie, climb; the way is free
  To higher things and higher."

The people raised uncertain sounds,
  Which through the air were sighing,
As they looked on with folded arms,
  " 'Tis no use, Davie, trying."
He placed his fingers in his ears,
  Impelled by warm desire,
And upwards through the mist arose
  To higher things and higher.

At last he reached the golden height
  With streaks of glory laden;
He gained the Lily of the Loch,
  The banker's matchless maiden.
He gained the honour of his race,
  Who bowed before his lyre.
Still Davie Drake this motto bears:
  "To higher things and higher."

MY AUTOBIOGRAPHY.

CHAPTER I.

EARLY LIFE.

AMES HOGG, the Ettrick Shepherd, has somewhat humorously said, "I like to write about myself: in fact, there are few things which I like better; it is so delightful to call up old reminiscences." So I have sat down to write about myself, and to enjoy some of the delight of which the Scotch poet speaks, in rambling in thought over long-forsaken tracts, and pleasantly musing through the dim aisles of the Past. If the simple record of my life-struggle should fail to interest the general reader, it may excite the attention of my patrons and friends, and stimulate the child of genius to patient perseverance; and its compilation will bring comfort to my own heart.

I was the eldest child of my parents, who, like the smitten patriarch in the land of Uz, were blest with seven sons and three daughters. One of my earliest recollections is a little white coffin, in which my eldest sister was carried to the grave. The place of my birth was a boulder-built cottage, with reedy roof, bare rafters, and clay floor, locally known as "Six Chimneys," on the top of Bolennowe Hill, Camborne, Cornwall, where I first saw the light on Saturday, October 14th, 1820. The rough house had no back door, nor any windows looking northward, except one about a foot square in the little pantry: but on the south side it had four windows, and a porch of primitive granite, literally small unpolished boulders. The wood-work of the roof was all visible, and sometimes the stars through the thatch; though my father was sure to have a thick layer of reed put on as the winter approached. There was no partition in the sleeping-room, which ran from one end of the building to the other. Nothing but the ruins of the old dwelling are now seen; for it fell in one of the winter storms about thirty years ago. The eastern end wall was much injured in my grandmother's time, through the explosion of a bag of gunpowder, which my uncle Matthew was foolishly drying before the fire. But the house now left standing beside it, however, is but a fair counterpart of itself.

My father's name was John, after whom I was called; and my mother was commonly called Kitty, though I believe her proper name was Christianna. She was the daughter of a farmer, named Smith, in the neighbouring village of Beacon, who kept his guineas on his bed-tester, and died before I was born. But my grandmother Smith I well remember, and believe her to be a godly woman. For a long time we visited the farm-house at Beacon annually, at the parish feast, when we generally dined off roast goose; and it was a wonderful luxury to me to turn the spit in the old parlour. At such times my uncles would tell stories, as we clustered around the November log; and one of them, whose name was Bill, and who had been in the French wars, much amused me with his accounts of sieges and shipwrecks. I have a dim recollection of finding on my grandmother Smith's shelf a very old book with the quaintest pictures; and I cannot divest myself of the thought that it was Dante's "Inferno." We continued to go to the farm-house, on the annual feast day, until my brothers and sisters became too numerous for my grandmother's table. We were also welcome visitors there at Christmas, when the great log smouldered on the chimney hearth, and the carol-singers came into the court. There was always plenty of good cheer, and tales told till the fire seemed to crackle with delight, and I caught whisperings which issued not from the ashes of the birch. How we loved to sleep in uncle's bed on Christmas Eve! That night our shoes were cleaned, and brightly blackened, taken upstairs with us, and placed just behind the bedcurtains where Old Father Christmas could not miss seeing them. We lay awake with bated breath and beating hearts, listening for his soft footstep up the stair, or down the rafters, until at last we fell asleep; and in the morning we were sure to find them stuffed full with sugar-candy, and other sweets. Childhood went, and we had passed out of boyhood before we could realize the fact that dear Old Father Christmas had not brought us our shoeful of sweet things. Of Santa Claus we knew nothing; it was all Old Father Christmas.

A singular story was often told me of my grandmother Smith going out of doors one summer night with but few clothes on. She wandered into their own fields, and cried bitterly as she went. She was in trouble, and trouble drove her to God. She looked at the bright stars as they twinkled overhead, and felt that their faces were kinder than those of her kindred. The green leaves trembled as the breeze passed by, and the flowers shed their delicious perfume upon the dews. No sound was heard save the rustling wind coming over the cornfields, and the solitary night-bird in the rushes. She stood by a granite stile where the ivy clung to the boulders, and the stone-crop clambered over the rocks, and wiped the tears from her face. And those tears did not fall unheeded in the darkness of the night; HE saw them who wept at the grave of Lazarus, and pitied the poor sufferer. Who can describe her thoughts at this moment, or the anguish of her wounded heart? She loved her Bible and her God, and knew where to take her sorrows. Lifting her hands to the starry firmament, she prayed to Him there, as she had often prayed in her stricken home, and the Lord heard her. Suddenly, she affirms, there was an angel with her. His face was bright as morning, and his long garments white as unsullied snow. His hair shone like gold, and there was more beauty in his person than pen can describe. He stood among the sleeping flowers with a light like a rainbow over his head. What he disclosed to her no one knows; but it was noticed that she was never so cast down with her domestic troubles afterwards. I have often rambled there in my boyhood, and stood wondering by the low stile where it is reported my grandmother saw the angel.

In addition to a small farm of seven or eight acres, which my father held on leasehold from W. W. Pendarves, Esq., he was also a copper miner, and was well known as a *tributer* in Dolcoath. He followed his daily avocation underground, and performed his farm-work in the evenings and mornings, and on holidays and leisurable opportunities. He was a diligent man, and a humble Christian. It may well be said of him that he studied but one book, and that book was the Bible. He expressed himself in few words, made no parade of his religion before his fellows, rarely engaged in any public duty, except occasionally offering prayer in his meeting in a cottage, and teaching a small class of boys in a Sunday school. Owing to the precarious nature of his employment in the mine, having only a certain portion of the mineral he discovered as his own share, his earnings were sometimes almost next to nothing, so that it was difficult to procure food for his household. During these times of solemn dearth I never heard him or my mother complain. She would often cheer him in the evenings, as we sat around the family board, with some word of encouragement, saying it would be better next week, or next month; and though I remained with my parents for twenty-five years, I never heard them speak disrespectfully, or even look angry at each other. They humbly walked in the fear of the Lord; and their gentle influence was sensibly felt by their household, all their children becoming members of Christian churches, and five of their sons preachers of the Gospel.

An autumn walk with my father when but a child is ever with me. Evening came on clear and quiet, without a cloud in the sky. We climbed our hill together, he leading me by the hand. Gaining its summit we paused, and looked upward. The firmament was covered with stars, shining in silvery splendour through the clear air. How brightly they beamed in their mystic orbits in the blue deeps of ether! And so near were we, standing on the crest of the mount, that in my childishness it seemed as if I could put forth my hand and touch them. The universe looked a bright palace of gems, where angels banqueted at the table of love. My infantile vision was riveted upon the scene, while the sparkling constellations flung their effulgence across the void. Suddenly my father, in a soft and solemn voice befitting the majesty of the moment, exclaimed, " God is the author of all this, my son: 'He made the stars also.'" This sweet parental love-lesson was never forgotten, nor did its influence ever decay.

When just entering on my teens, my father, for what cause I cannot now remember, had to use severity with me. He took me into the stone-paved court before the house, where I received his chastisement with a rod. I remember his look of sorrow, and still seem to hear his sighs, and to feel his hand upon my shoulder. The elder-tree at the end of the house looked down upon me with warning eyes, and the prying sparrows upon the thatch became my judges. No one knows how poignantly I felt it; and I resolved that he should never have an occasion to repeat it, and he never did. Although our house was so situated that we could see the North and South Channels from the highest point of the hill, yet I was nearly ten years old before I was near the sea. Then, on a holiday, my father took me and my brother William to the sands of Gwithian, travelling on foot forth and back. I shall never forget the impression made upon my mind when I first drew near the great ocean, beheld the huge cliffs and rocks, and heard the thunder of the billows upon the shore. I saw it afterwards in my dreams, and heard its eternal roll among the daisies and lark-bursts of my mountain meads.

My aunt Margery, I have reason to believe, was remarkably pious, and her love for private prayer was proverbial. When I was very young she was much attached to me, and I was frequently her willing companion. She led me among the mosses, and talked to me where the primroses bloomed. Knitting was her chief occupation, which she diligently pursued, whilst I often sat at her feet charmed with the click of her shining needles. She had stated times for prayer, not only at mornings and evenings, but also about three o'clock in the afternoons. Across the kitchen was placed an unpainted deal form, which was very coarsely made, with rounded edges and rounded legs, and here she bent at her devotions. She often had me with her, and I knelt down by her side, placing my small hands on the rude seat, whilst she poured out her heart in fervent supplications to Him who seeth in secret, and who rewardeth openly. Through the mists of sixty years I still see that old deal form in the middle of my grandmother's kitchen, with my praying aunt kneeling beside it, while the sparrows chattered outside on the shaven reed, and the robin sang his hymn of thanksgiving on the open hatch. Nor can I doubt her simple prayers have been answered on my behalf as fully and as freely as if they were offered in the grandest cathedral.

The little farm which my father rented on Bolennowe Hill was one which my grandfather, Ben Harris, had redeemed from the wild. He must have laboured hard to do this, as the huge boulders in the rude wide hedges testify. These hedges were a great delight to me in my boyhood, covered with moss and ivy, where ferns held forth their beautiful fronds, whortleberries throve abundantly, and the golden bells of the gorse made delicious music. I was soon confirmed in the belief that fays and fairies thronged there in the moonlight, and strangely-tinselled genii dwelt among the stones. The summer winds that gently floated along brought poetry to my ears; and even the hurricane of winter taught my muse to sing. Young as I was, I could hear the magic of music everywhere; and I played among the boulders with the angel of song at my side.

I cannot recollect ever seeing my grandfather but once, and then death took him away. My brother William and I were building a little twig-house in a corner of the garden, when mother gently came and told us that he was dead. He was a tall old man, wearing a wide-rimmed hat; and I still seem to see the polished buckles on his shoes, and the shining buttons on his Quaker-cut coat. It is not at all probable that he ever indulged much in poetry or the poets, or knew that such a man as William Shakespere had ever existed. It is said that a neighbour lent him Milton's "Paradise Lost." On returning it, he was asked how he liked it; and his reply is characteristic of his non-acquaintance with this unexampled production—"The man that wrote that book ought to be hanged!" What he would have said of his grandson and his rustic rhymes I cannot tell; perhaps he would have doomed him to imprisonment for life. In all my boy-searches over my grandmother's dwelling, I do not remember discovering any books; so I conclude that my grandfather contrived to grope along his darksome way pretty much without them. One of his sayings, however, contains such a fair share of moral philosophy that it should not be omitted here. When gently chided for some strange act of supposed indifference, he calmly gazed into his accuser's face and deliberately replied, "Thee show me a man without a fault, and I will show thee a man without a head." I have tried, but cannot trace back our ancestry any farther, and know not whether my grandfather was a Saxon or a Celt. This I know, that when the little farm which he enclosed from the common, on the death of my father, which took place on Sunday, April 23, 1848, accelerated by a fall in the mine, fell into the lord's hands, the steward refused to renew my mother's lease, heeding not the orphan or the widow's tears. The consequence was that she had to leave the farm, dispose of her little stock, and retire with her six children to a small house at the foot of the hill, to struggle through life as best she might. The farm was left untaken for two years afterwards, unploughed and untilled, the rent set upon it by the steward being more than it was worth.

Of my grandmother Joan, on my father's side, I remember but little. She wore what is generally known as a "Friend's" bonnet, and was commonly attired in a red cloak. I do not think she was at all given to reading, though I believe she was a Christian woman. She kept a goat or two, which she often milked at her door under the great elder-tree; and I cannot forget the rich flavour of the cream the milk produced. I often watched them feeding from her hand, when in a very gentle voice, which I still seem to hear, she taught me the lesson of kindness. Her garden contained beds of choice herbs, which she used to dry and preserve in paper bags, hanging them in the great chimney. She kept the walls of her room whitewashed, and the clay floor well sanded; and the shining pewter plates on the dresser-shelves had a great attraction for me. On her return from market or shop I was sure to steal into her room, our house being next door, to receive my accustomed packet of sweets, and a piece of hot heavy potato-cake baked in the ashes. As I ate the crisp cake, and listened to the music of the crackling furze and heath under the pot, the click of her needles as she sat by the hot embers, and her enchaining story as wild as our own hills, I felt sure that I had the dearest, kindest grandmother in all the world. A small cutting of the elder, under which my grandmother Joan used to milk her goats, was brought with us to Falmouth, and planted in a corner of our little garden. It is now grown into a large tree, where the sparrows come for their breakfast of berries in the autumn; though it never bore any fruit at the end of my father's house. As it now gently waves in the evening light, it often reminds me of the mountain goats and my grandmother Joan.

The next house to my father's was occupied by a ploughman named John Eustace. When very small, I was standing with his wife and daughter by the roadside. An old bent beggar passed by, when the little girl exclaimed, "Mother, can you see!" He stopped upon his crutches, turned his bearded face towards us, and sharply replied, "Can you see! Ay, and what can you see? A poor old man in a bundle of rags? I have been in places where I have seen the KING, and he never said, 'Can you see?'" The old man and his words were not to be forgotten. One morning I entered our neighbour's house. Hearing no one below, I mounted the stairs, and in an old box in a back room discovered a lantern-ring. This struck my child-fancy: I stretched forth my hand and took it. But I felt it was wrong, and before I had reached the bottom of the stairs I wished it back again. The counsel of my Christian mother was in my mind, and the very birds and winds seemed mocking me with earnest voices. I played with it for a while, but its charms grew less and less, until its very sight disgusted me; nor could I rest until I cautiously crept back to the low chamber and deposited it in the box.

Another incident I cannot forget. I could not have been then more than four or five years old. I left my mother's door, and by some contrivance got over the stile at the end of the house leading into the meadow. Here I played among the daisies and clover for some time, pulling off the great heads of the ox-eye, and collecting moss-cups and ivy-leaves from the hedges. So intent was I on my botanical selection, that I noticed not the sinking sun, or the rising moon, until the falling twilight warned me it was time to return to the house. But this was not so easy as leaving it. Round and round I walked, still getting more bewildered and farther into the gloom. Then I sat down on a rock by the side of the path in the Water Field, shut my eyes and sobbed. Over me were the broad heavens, studded with stars, and around me the stillness and the solemness of night. My parents, alarmed at my absence, sought for me with many fears; and when they found me, I was sitting upon this mossy boulder, sobbing forth at intervals, "There is nobody here but I and the *buckaw*." The buckaw was a supposed pixey that haunted the neighbourhood.

Every new year's morning, the first act of my mother was to go to the rick of turf, bring in a dry sod, and deposit it in the woodcorner. What her reason was for doing this I cannot say, except that she wished her first item of labour to be something useful. When the sun-rays streaked the east, and gilded the summit of our hill, we knew it was time to rise, and so we got out of bed. When day was done, and murky twilight wrapt the earth in her shroud, we all gathered around the fireside, read a portion of some interesting volume, and retired to rest as peacefully as the dear little redbreast in the bush. In the morning we were often aroused from our slumber by the shrill voice of a boy going to his work in the mine, who, at the corner of our garden, called to his blithe companions. When we heard his cheerful halloo, it was exactly time to get up, and he it was who was our alarum clock. Peace to his memory! May his career be a happy one, and may he remember in the full blaze of his glory how, when crowing to his comrades in his boyish glee, he startled a drowsy poet from his golden dreams. The first thing I often saw, when I opened my eyes in the morning dusk, was my father with flint and steel and tinder-box trying to kindle a light. When his duties pressed him to rise more early than usual, the barn-door cock had his roost made in the woodcorner of the old kitchen under the stairs, whose shrill crowing aroused us before the breaking of the dawn.

My aunt Catherine, whose parents lived in a one-chimneyed house on the downs, not far from Hangman Barrow, where we were told a crock of guineas lay under the stones, sometimes came to see us. On one occasion she brought me a little book which greatly interested me. Amongst its contents was the well-known allegory:—For want of a nail the shoe was lost, for want of a shoe the horse was lost, for want of a horse the rider was lost, being overtaken and slain by the enemy: all for want of a horseshoe nail. The sad image of the unfortunate horseman, so miserably left to his fate, continually haunted me; and the lesson of promptly attending to little things was not lost. And how often my gentle mother charmed me in the light of the sputtering furze-brand, as we clustered around her knees in the dear old kitchen, and she told us tales of the long-ago, when men loved virtue more than gold, and simpleness and truth were unalloyed gems. Sitting by the old hearth-stone where my grandfather had sat before me, and another generation had mused and passed away, I listened to her loving stories with wondering joy. She told of hallowed deeds performed in secret, which, like angels of mercy, shed a halo over the weeping world. She told of Beauty pining in solitude, and Virtue neglected in the humble shed. She told of good men in rags, and wicked men in princely habiliments. She told of sorrow and suffering as the lot of all, and of Him who came to redeem the world. And as I listened my young heart beat, and imagination bore me away on her dazzling wings. Her loving spirit did much to people the realm of fancy with fairy forms, so that it was but a few steps from her knees into the land of enchantment. Whatever truth my homely strains may possess is greatly owing to my mother.

Almost as soon as I was able to walk and use my tongue, my father led me on Sundays, when the weather was fine, to the chapel in the village of Troon, where he was accustomed to worship, which was about a mile from our house on the hill. Our path lay chiefly through the meadows; and it was very pleasant to me to watch the birds and butterflies, and listen to the hum of the bees among the flowers. The solemn silence of the Sabbath rested on my child-spirit, and I would fain believe that God and angels came nearer to earth on that holy day. I sat quite still in the little chapel, and heard through the minister the voice of God speaking to the people. I have revived these early church-going walks in the following verses, which have just been written.

> The Gothic window where I sit
>   Looks out upon the moor,
> And Autumn's hand has thickly strewn
>   The dry leaves at our door.

But o'er the hills I dimly see
  Another golden morn,
When father led me by the hand
  Through fields of waving corn.

The path was narrow which we walked,
  With daisies in the sod,
And cheerfully we travelled on
  Towards the house of God.
I hear the larks again to-day
  Above the flowering thorn,
When father led me by the hand
  Through fields of waving corn.

The hedges showed unnumbered gems,
  Which Flora scattered there,
And every breeze that murmured by
  Was wooing us to prayer.
The blooms are here which then I saw
  My native meads adorn,
When father led be by the hand
  Through fields of waving corn.

The bench was lowly where we sat
  To hear the preacher pray,
Unbacked, uncushioned, roughly planed,
  Yet tears were wiped away.
And thankful was my childish heart,
  Not then with sorrow torn,
That father led me by the hand
  Through fields of waving corn.

And thanks to Him I render now,
  Beneath life's evening skies,
And praises throng my grateful lips,
  And tears are in mine eyes,
For mercies from the God of Love,
  New every eve and morn,
That father led me by the hand
  Through fields of waving corn.

Six years had scarcely passed, when my brother and I, without the consent of our parents, went to fish in the nearest stream. It was the month of March, and still cold. I remember it as if it only transpired a week ago. A few primroses were smiling under the banks, and the golden blossoms of the gorse-bushes were just beginning to show themselves. Now and then a lark soared into the ether, and we shaded our eyes with our hands to watch it and hear its song. But we were not happy, having gone without leave. We caught an exceedingly large trout, and in doing so wet ourselves to the skin. Evening was approaching, and I asked my brother to go home. He seemed stupified in his drenched garments, and did not care to move, so I took him by the hand and led him up the hill. In this way we reached the outer hedge of my father's farm, and then he suddenly stopped, lay down upon a bank, and begged me to let him sleep. Young as I was, I knew he was seized with cold, and that if left alone he must die. So I took him on my back, though I could scarcely trudge under him, and went on. The ground was slippery and steep, and I had hedges to go over with my unconscious burden, which seemed to grow heavier at every step. The stars came out, the light from our window gleamed over the meadow, and soon I delivered him into my mother's arms. Warm blankets were procured, the fire replenished, cordials administered, and shortly my brother was himself again. By God's blessing I had saved his life. A few evenings afterwards we were to bear the punishment due to us for thus going a-fishing without leave, by retiring supperless to bed. But as we lay awake listening to the old clock on the top of the stairs, and sadly sobbing by turns, we heard the softest footfall on the chamber floor, and knew it was our mother stealing in to us with some thick slices of bread and butter. She could not bear to think of our going to sleep hungry.

At the end of our house on the hill was a rude arch, composed of rough blocks of granite, the top of which was covered with green turf. This we called "The Mountain;" and when a child I frequently climbed to the top, and sat there alone with the great world bathed in beauty around me. The sky, and clouds, and blushing flowers, the solitary hawthorn on the croft hedge, the birds floating through the clear azure, the ruffle of the reeds, and the murmur of the brooklet in the valley delighted my simple soul, and filled me with thoughts I could not express. Nature was then teaching me some of her fairest lessons, which after years would more fully unravel.

Our parish feast, which was held on the nearest Sunday to the eleventh of November, was a high time with us. We anticipated its annual return with great delight, making it the subject of conversation both morning and evening as we sat around the great chimney fire, my mother mending our worn garments, and my patient, industrious father cobbling our boots and shoes after his return from the mine. They would sometimes join in our remarks, well-pleased to see their children happy. A lamb, or a small mountain sheep, was commonly killed for the occasion, my father being then his own butcher. A relative or two sometimes joined us, one of the most important being my uncle George Smith, who generally brought his flute with him. He was a bachelor, and as such he lived and died. How we watched the process of cooking none but country boys can know; and we concluded that our mother was the best provider in England. The collation was always served up in the old hall, where we were all arranged in order; and we had a more sumptuous dinner on that occasion than on any other day throughout the year. These festive seasons became my earliest subjects for verse, and several of those rustic jingles may be found in my published works, though the greater number have been destroyed after reading them over once or twice to my admiring brothers and sisters. A halo rested on these far-off days, the golden glow of which flickers through the silence of the present hours.

A singular story is told of my uncle George, who, it is said, was much too fond of the drink-cup. On one occasion he saddled his horse, and, arrayed in yellow top-boots and spurs, rode off to a neighbouring tavern. Here he drank too much toddy, and stayed too long with the chatty landlord. It was a moonlight night, and the horse, knowing much better than his master, brought him home into the farm-yard, and stopped by the side of the glistening gutter. It was a large, deep pool, which would not have been suffered to remain so near the house in these sanitary reform days. The drunk man foolishly supposed that he was by his bedside; so he stript to his shirt, went into the gutter and lay down. When the green, muddy water gurgled over him, his lost reason partially returned, and he shrieked like a coward who meets some grim shadow in the dark. He tore out of the horse-pond, and rushed up the road he knew not whither. The first house he came to was a little thatched hovel by the wayside, where he knocked loudly at the door. The sleeping inhabitant was aroused; and the sight and smell which greeted her could not easily have been forgotten. A few kind words restored the inebriate to something like sanity, and he crept back to his own dwelling leaving a dark gutter-trail behind him. O how very low the dreadful drink pulls down its victim!. This unfortunate episode supplied me with Fardo, one of the characters in Bulo.

I could not have been more than four or five years old when I first went to the Sunday school where my father was a teacher, and derived much Christian knowledge under the godly superintendence of Mr. John Thomas, who was a thoroughly educated man. Soon after this a revival of religion took place in the village; and at a meeting for children in a cottage, whilst on my knees praying, a holy sensation filled my being, the like of which I have never felt before or since. My lips were unsealed, so that I loudly praised the name of the Lord; and so buoyant was I, that I thought I could almost fly away. I embraced my father and mother and all I met, telling them that I was mercifully visited by the Spirit, and that He had made me His child. But this state of feeling was of very brief duration, though the remembrance of it often comforted me. When about sixteen, I became a teacher in the school, and rose from one post to another until I filled the office of librarian. Though my week days were so busily and so hardly occupied, I felt it to be my duty to devote the Sabbath to the service of the Master. So I soon became connected with two schools, being superintendent of one at Black Rock, which was in the midst of a barren moor, in the parish of Crowan, about two miles from my Troon-Moor home. It was a very uncultivated district, with scarcely a green meadow to be seen from the little chapel-door; and morally and intellectually it was no better—boys and girls in their teens not knowing the letters of the alphabet. In addition to these morning and afternoon duties, I frequently had to preach twice on a Sunday, finishing my labours about ten o'clock at night. This course of rather severe Sabbath discipline was cheerfully pursued almost up to the time that I became a Scripture Reader at Falmouth, in August, 1857.

There were six hawthorns, very far apart, on the hedges of my father's grounds. They were very stunted trees, smitten with the winds that swept over the hill, and though they seldom blossomed or bore fruit, yet they were great favourites of mine. Under them I used to sit entranced with the music of the breeze through the branches, reading a book, or writing my rhymes to the sound of the cuckoo on the bank. They have frequently been made the subjects of my verse; and in a recent effusion I have sung of one of them as follows:—

> There is a hawthorn in my father's croft,
>   Where oft a stripling prayed,
> When twilight deepened, and the winds were soft,
>   And murmurs filled the glade.
>
> The stars beheld him from their homes of blue,
>   The clouds with crimson spread,
> The latest bird that swiftly homeward flew,
>   The mystery overhead.
>
> The moonbeams kissed the tears upon his face,
>   Which like clear crystal shine,
> As sighed he softly in that solemn place,
>   "O God, my heart is Thine!"
>
> The rocks around him were his temple-walls,
>   The mountain-top his shrine,
> His organ-peal, the tiny waterfalls,
>   That murmured hymns Divine.
>
> His audience, angels floating near and far,
>   His music, bubbling springs,
> His silvery lamps, the moon and evening star,
>   His priest, the King of kings.
>
> And forth that stripling went from year to year,
>   Walking the homeward way,
> With trusting meekness humbleness and fear,
>   Until his locks were grey.
>
> Yet still behind the slopes where childhood strayed,
>   And buds and blossoms be,
> And music murmured from each grassy glade,
>   He sees that old thorn tree.

CHAPTER II.
GOING TO THE MINE.

HEN came my first journey down the hill to Dame Trezona's school in the hamlet of Bolennowe under the trees, where I sat upon a low cricket at her feet to learn the A B C. She had some half-a-dozen boys and girls in all; and I was soon considered to be the best scholar in her establishment. I do not remember much about her at this far distance, only that she had reddish hair gathered under a high cap, that she wore spectacles and a cotton bedgown, and took snuff. I made fair proficiency in all the scholastic arts she could inculcate, and soon became very fond of books. My father presented me with a penny Robinson Crusoe with a rude frontispiece, which

I carried to my bedchamber with me every night. This was my first book, except the school primer, which I could really call my own. About this time a ragged copy of Burns's "Cotter's Saturday Night" fell into my hands, which I found on an old shelf in my mother's kitchen, where a store of rich trifles in my boyish eyes lay among the dust and cobwebs, and which I read with great avidity over and over again, until I could pretty well understand its meaning in the Scotch dialect. Other books of rhyme helped to kindle within me the love of song, which Nature fostered amid the brakes and boulders of my native hill. The evenings of my boyhood were evenings of purest joy. Cowering by the old grate, in the dim firelight which clothed the walls in shadowy warriors and plumed knights mounted on floating steeds, I hung over the "Pilgrim's Progress" until I seemed to behold the gladdened travellers in the land of Beulah, and to hear the bells of the city of God.

I did not continue very long under the tuition of Dame Trezona, but entered a similar institution kept by a woman named Penpraze, which was held in Troon Chapel. She, and several of her scholars, were much alarmed on one occasion duing a hail-storm in summer, accompanied with lightening and thunder, when some of the glass was broken, though I felt but little fear. Leaving her and the old edifice, I was placed under the care of a harsh pedagogue, whose name, I believe, was Reed. He had a great number of boys under his charge, some of whom, I suppose, were unruly enough. But his discipline was singularly severe. After seeing him strike my companion's palm with a flat piece of hard wood studded thickly with sharp nails, so that every point brought the blood, I felt disheartened, and begged to be sent to some other academy. He was a genuine counterpart of old Squeers, whom Dickens has described so graphically. Is it any wonder that the pupils of such ungainly punchers should leave the dreaded enclosure dunces and blockheads? A few days under his savagery sufficed for me; and I have quite forgotten his appearance, except that he had a bald head, small eyes, and wore glasses over a very wide, red nose.

My next teacher was a miner, a mild pious man, of the name of Roberts. He had met with an accident in his work underground, depriving him of a leg, which was badly supplied with a wooden stump. In those days any shattered being wrecked in the mill or the mine, if he could read John Bunyan, count fifty backwards, and scribble the squire's name, was considered good enough for a pedagogue; and when he could do nothing else, was established behind a low desk in a school. I do not think John Roberts's acquirements extended far beyond reading, writing, and arithmetic; and I doubt if he knew what the word geography meant. The School Board was then a name not found in the English vocabulary. His seminary was a thatched house by the road-side, in a poorly-cultivated district, known as Forest Gate, which has long since disappeared. It was, perhaps, a mile from our house, and our way to it led over the moor, where I have often lingered to hear the babble of the brook, and the song of the sirens among the withes. Here I improved myself in reading, and learnt to write and spell, and to experience the puzzle of figures as far as the multiplication of money, leaving all other branches of knowledge to slumber in forgetfulness. But though John Roberts was a stranger to most of the sciences now so generally taught in the schools, he possessed what, perhaps, is better still —a thorough knowledge of the saving power of the Gospel of Jesus Christ. His daily instructions began and ended with extempore prayer. This influence for good could not fail to have been felt by his pupils; and it yet lives in reedy hamlets and smoky cities to brighten the moral world.

I do not remember ever being kept in school but once after the other scholars were dismissed. Then my writing was so very bad that John Roberts was obliged to be severe with me. I knew the fault was more in the miserably poor pen than in myself. Of course, we all wrote with quills; for this was before steel pens were invented. I took the old ink-stained stump up to the master's desk, and tremblingly asked him if he would kindly repair it. He did so at once; and I went back to my place and commenced my task. The twilight descended, and I thought of my mother and brothers at home sitting around the supper board and wondering where I could be. But my pen was not like the same, it glided over the sheet most beautifully, so that my copy looked as if it were done by some other hand.

AN INCIDENT OF MY SCHOOL DAYS.

John Roberts was vastly pleased, and I was never more kept in from that evening. Thus good tools often make good workmen. I cannot tell whether I celebrated this event in rhyme: if I did, it fell with the falling of the old thatched house on Bolennowe Hill.

During one of my school-boy rambles I strayed into a neighbour's meadows not far from my father's house. It was in the early spring, and my object was to gather wild flowers, of which I was so very fond. I secured a tolerably large number, consisting of violets, primroses, blue-bells, and daisies, with a sprinkling of buttercups and clover. The sun was hot, and I was thirsty. Seeing a reed-covered cottage in a corner of one of the fields, I made up to the door. As I drew near I heard sounds within, as of two people conversing together. I stood on the threshold, and asked for a drink of water. Three times I asked, as the conversation seemed to go on, but no one heeded me. The door being open, I entered; and there was the good man of the dwelling quite alone in his humble room, kneeling in earnest prayer before a low form. His hands were lifted, and his face turned upwards; and so absorbed was he in his devotions, so earnestly pleading with Jehovah, that, though I repeatedly asked him for a drink of water, he never answered me, or dropped his eyes from the vision of glory which he surely beheld. I turned and left him at his devotions, bearing his image in my soul. His was true worship; and the example of this good man was not lost, I trust, upon me.

I have previously alluded to my father and his evening shoe-mending. This was done after his long daily toil in the mine and in the fields. Here he sat on a low stool in the old hall, cobbling away as patiently as the angler by the brook-side, until the clock on the top of the stairs struck ten, and his drowsy offspring crept off to bed. This he did repeatedly evening after evening, so that he rarely had time to look into a book. Six wild boys racing over the highlands brought him no small task for leather and nail. A cobbler was never hired, he sitting to his labour from January until June, and from June until January came again. Seeing I was so fond of books and study, he sometimes appeared to dislike it, saying he did not think I should ever earn my living. Why he said it puzzles me, because I did my farm-work farther forth than any of my brothers, not neglecting any labour-duty for song, which course I have strictly followed until the present hour. But his patient image is still before me as he used to sit hour after hour on the low seat in the old hall, with a ragged boot or shoe between his knees, awl and end in hand, whilst I silently crouched in the light of the blazing furze-brand, happily pencilling my early hymns to the beat of his cobbling-hammer.

My first attempts at rhyme were made whilst I was a scholar under my one-legged miner-master; and my verses were written on the blank spaces of my first ciphering book. For years this was treasured up as an interesting trophy where the coy Muses set their earliest mark, until its fate was sealed by neglect and the damps and decays of time. What became of it I cannot tell, unless it was made into boats by my brothers, and ferried across the carn pool. Having discovered the secret of rhyme, and the mystery of inventing couplets, I found it impossible to stop. Wherever I went my harp was with me. The love of song grew with my physical growth, and was dearer to me than the smile of friendship. I wrote in the dear old chimney by the winter firelight, while my buxom brothers were shouting around me. And this was my only study, save the barn or the cow-house. O how I longed for some obscure corner, where, with a handful of fire in the grate, and the smallest lamp upon the unplaned board, I might write my hymns in quiet. But this was denied me, and I often sat in my bed-room, with my feet wrapped in my mother's cloak, with a pair of small bellows for my writing-desk. And in the brown autumn-time, when a pensive calm pervades the woods, and a solemn rustle is heard upon the hills, I sometimes made ink to write my idyls with the juice of blackberries which grew on the hedges of our mountain meads. Paper, too, was a scarce commodity, and so I used the clean side of cast-off labelled tea-wrappers, which my mother would bring from the shop. Very often my juvenile attempts were destroyed with my own hands; but when I concluded that my performances were more happily conceived, I read them to my brothers and playfellows, who declared they were grandeur itself.

Very early in boyhood I remember having been sent to the the town of Camborne with a basket for paint for my father. I was told how much to bring; and the exact money, wrapped in a piece of brown paper, was put in my pocket. I reached the shop known as "Saddler Dick's," and with a palpitating heart approached the counter. A not very pleasant-looking lame man was behind it, and with a faltering voice I asked, "Please for two pounds of paint." He looked hard at me, saying, "Who is it for?" "My father," I replied. "Is your father a carpenter?" asked he. "No," I answered. "Then I do not think you were told to ask for two pounds," said he. "Yes I was," I replied excitedly, "I am sure of it. It is to paint a wheelbarrow, and the barn-door, and our cart. O, I am quite sure of it." The paint was weighed up, and the coarse jug placed in the basket. Then I produced the money wrapped in the brown paper packet, and laid it on the counter, the top of which was about level with my chin. He counted it: and what was my astonishment and chagrin to find that it was exactly the sum for one pound of paint! "Ah!" he exclaimed, looking at me with severity, "I thought so! You are too positive, too positive," and I turned my face homewards a wiser, though a humbler, boy. But no rhymes would visit my brain for days afterwards.

I little thought when in boyhood I used to wander alone to the top of Carnmenellis to gather wood anemonies among the carved rocks, and to write my verses where the long lichen waved on the boulders, that the struggle to succeed would be so severe. All the hills around my father's dwelling found in me an eager climber, when I read the lichened pillars around their granite doorways with delighted eyes. But the longest and most feathery lichen I found on Carnmenellis, specimens of which frequently adorned our parlour mantle-piece, and the shelves of my mother's dresser. Carn Brea, too, was often my favourite resort, where there are so many evident traces of the Druids, and the numerous rock-basins are a charm to Cornwall. I sang of its castle and its crags in rhymes which only lived to tingle for the briefest span in the ears of my companions. But in fancy now I often tread the narrow sheep-paths along its mossy sides, where my favourite heather grew so abundantly, before the heavy monument crowned its shaggy summit, or a smoking mine-stack marred its beauty. With my harp resting upon the turf, and a huge shelf of granite over me, where the poor blind devotees have often performed their unholy rites, I have gazed across the sounding moorland on my native residence, the shaven eaves of which had power to move my spirit more than the gables of the grandest mansion, and where the lark of melody sang for ever.

A brisk walk of about two hours brought me to Tregoning Hill, where I got a more distinct view of the Cornish Mount. This unattractive elevation has also been the subject of my rhymes, which have long been lost in the tide of years. On one occasion, in summer, I entered a cottage at its foot to solicit a cup of cold water. An old bent crone occupied the kitchen, with a face wrinkled, though truly pleasant. We had an earnest conversation, and she told me a long list of her troubles. She was evidently pleased to have an attentive listener, which I could see in her sparkling eyes as she glanced over her metal spectacles. I was then a little more than twenty-seven. Looking earnestly at me, she enquired, "How old are you?" "What age do you suppose I might be?" I asked. She adjusted her glasses to give me a piercing scrutiny, and then exclaimed in a shrill, squeaking voice, "Well, I should think you were about fifty!" I closed her door, and ruminated on my antique appearance all the way homeward.

At nine years of age I was taken from school and put to work in the fields, to drive the horses in the plough to Uncle George Harris, Bolennowe. I was then barely able to read and write and cast up figures. My master was a tall bony man, with low forehead and heavy grey eyes, who had more faith in the ghosts of the beacon than the virtue of books. His arms were remarkably long, swinging by his side like the branches of some old tree. His two horses were called Bob and Fly, which were animals really worthy of a photograph. Bob was grey, and Fly was red; and a constant utterance of Uncle George was, as I held the whip in one hand, and the halter of the nearest horse in the other, "Smither, Bob, Fly." He had no wife, but a wide-backed, dumpy housekeeper, named Rosy, who would never walk more than two or three steps before she turned to look around her. I was quite interested in the bright pewter plates on the dresser-shelves, and not less so in the cold meat which we regularly had for dinner on Mondays, with the hot potatoes roasted in the peat ashes on the hearth. I have frequently stood to watch Uncle George cutting turf on the common, which was adjoining my father's croft. He would cut one turf and rest upon his tool-handle, taking a strict survey of the surrounding country. Then he would cut another turf and do the same, and so on throughout the summer day. He was my father's butcher, and always killed our fat pigs, when he was attired in a blue frock. This was a great day with me, for I had to assist in boiling the water in the wide chimney, stuffing blazing furze and heather under the huge copper pan. How often have I got up in the early morning, ere the sparrows had left the eaves, or the robin his mossy shelter by the bank, to watch the wondrous preparations for this important event, delighted with the sputter and sparkle of the moorland fuel, and reading hymns of happiness in the rainbow-coloured flames. The heavy cake followed, baked in the ashes. I do not recollect writing any rhymes whilst with Uncle George, partly because I was kept so busy, and partly because I was only with him for a few months; nor do I remember whether I had any payment in the shape of wages for the long day's work, save the dinner of cold meat and roasted potatoes.

I then went to work with an old tin-streamer of the name of Waters. One day we discovered a Jews'-house in the bog. The tin had run over their smelting-pot, and had lodged in the turf, which had occurred, it is supposed, hundreds of years before the birth of Christ. The next day we took our find in a cart to Hayle, and he realized for it, if I remember rightly, £37. The old tin-streamer gave me threepence a day to throw sand from the river in Forest Moor. Here I stood with bare feet in the running water, with a small shovel in my hands, and ate my dinner in a peat-built rush-covered hut. The tinkle of the crystal brooks, the sigh of the wind through the white tufted rushes, the birds singing on the willow branches, or floating carelessly through the clear air, revived the suppressed spirit of numbers never again to sink into repose. I wrote for my companions, and felt richly repaid with their honest praises under the flowery hawthorn, when the white moon rose over the hamlet, and the returning mower's whistle sounded in the hollow. These lines were rude and rustic enough, none of which I can remember; and they were sometimes embellished with pen-and-ink drawings of my own, and were considered superior to anything ever produced by mortal man. So strangely did the power of composition assail me, that I would leave my companions at their pleasant games, and steal away to my favourite bower, where I sat alone among the heather till the twilight deepened, and the weird boulders caught the glitter of the stars and the music of the evening winds. On my right hand the Nine Maidens stood motionless on the moor; on my left were the Druid-relics, rock-basins, and ancient castle of Carn Brea; before me were green fields and tree-covered hamlets; behind me, the rugged rifts of the Land's End; below me, the clear river in the rushes, and above me the illimitable sky with its eternity of love. So far away from the noise and clamour of towns and cities, the rush of commerce, and the roar of the manufactory, it is scarcely any wonder that I was held in the spell of song. The great granite rocks, silent in their loneliness; the weird tracks along the mossy moorland, trod by fairy feet; the miles of rustling heather, where the plover and partridge found a safe shelter; the trickling streams tumbling among the stones, the lights and shadows that fell upon the plain, and the rhyme-laden whispers falling down the distant heights, had more poetic power for my yearning heart than all the rigour and regime of books or schools.

The construction of my bower, to which allusion is frequently made in my verses, was fashioned by a wide ditch, which was dug up to fill in a hedge parting a meadow from our under croft. A piece of the virgin turf, about two feet wide, was left standing close to the foundation, and this served me as a pleasant seat. It was covered with soft moss and thyme, and large tufts of heather hung over me from the hedge-top and sides. To this place of Divine inspiration I always retreated when I had an hour of my own, as it was only a few hundred yards from our cottage porch, sometimes with a book, but oftener with my pencil and paper, hearing sounds and seeing shapes which are so alien to the multitude. The swallows wheeled around me, floating down the hill-side over gorse-brakes and thyme-banks where fays frolicked unseen, now low, now high, and then back again on their arrowy flight, so that their wings sometimes almost fanned my flowing hair. Not a sound disturbed the solitude, save the clear river in the valley, or the last lay of the lark among the crimson clouds. It was the undisturbed realm of contemplation, where Gentleness and Truth walked arm-in-arm. The golden bells of the heather, gently touched by the fingers of the wind, made music in my ears, which travels with me down the vale of time to die not till I lie down in my last sleep. The hare-bells grew there, and the graceful ferns, which taught me lessons I can never repeat, though I strive to unravel them again and again. A solitary hawthorn stood not far off, around which ever floated the tenderest numbers, brought to me by the breezes in my meditative hall. I long for it now, though I know I cannot see it any more; for the ruthless hand of time has entirely changed it. The plough has been over the croft, and oats and hay now wave on the borders of my bower.

At ten years of age my father took me with him to Dolcoath Mine, to work on the surface, in assisting to dress and prepare copper ore for the market. Sometimes I had to work at the keeve,* sometimes at the picking-table, sometimes in the slide, sometimes on the floors, sometimes in the cobbing-house, and sometimes at the hutch. Sometimes I had to wheel the mineral in a barrow until the skin came off my hands, and my arms were deadened with the heavy burden. Sometimes I was scorched with the sun until I almost fainted; and then I was wet with the rains of heaven so that I could scarcely put one foot before another. I left my home at six in the morning, and returned to it again at six in the evening. Yet I never complained, nor would I if the same sharp scene had to be enacted again. God had placed me there, and I knew it was right. And,

---

* See Glossary at the end of the volume.

moreover, I had the song-angel to comfort me, walking at my side among the mineral-splinters, rocks and rubbish, and whispering in the narrow lanes and grassy meadows as I travelled homewards sweeter utterances than language can reveal. On my way to and from the scene of my labours through long lanes bramble-covered, and over meadows snowy with daisies, or by hedges blue with hyacinths, or over whispering carnes redolent with the hum of bees, the beautiful world around me teemed with syllables of song.

When not more than twelve years old, I used frequently to repeat the rhymes I had written to my mates in the mine. They would put me to stand on a hand-barrow by the cobbing-house door, or on a heap of mineral on the floors, and then gather around me to hear my verses. Old men with grey locks, boys with sparkling eyes, and maidens with cheeks a-flame would listen with wonder, entranced with the spell of my song. And it was not unpleasant to me to hear them conversing with each other, while the jingle of my last lay was in their ears, "What a wonderful boy that is! he can read a book like a parson." These rambling rhymes have been destroyed long ago, and my admiring audience is scattered to congregate no more to the echo of my faltering lute. But I warmly thank their shadows for this the first breath of praise.

After toiling in this way for two years, my father took me with him into the interior of the earth, nearly two hundred fathoms under the surface. Ascending and descending the ladders, some sixty or seventy in number, was a fearful task. On my first descent into the mine, when I was about thirteen years of age, my father went before with a rope fastened to his waist, the other end of which was attached to my trembling self. If my hands and feet slipped from the rounds of the ladder, perhaps my father might catch me, or the sudden jerk might pull us both into the darkness to be bruised to death on the rocks. Sometimes the ladder went down through the middle of a huge cavern, warping and shaking at every step, and with the candle stuck to my hat-crown I could not see from side to side. Sometimes they slanted one way, sometimes another; and sometimes we had to climb over craggy rocks crashed into the void, where a slip of the foot would be our doom. And when at last we reached our working place, a huge cell in the hollowed rock, I looked up in boyish expectation to see the moon and stars, and was quite disappointed to find nothing but the blackest gloom. Foolishly I took up a small stone to see if I could strike the far-away roof, which rebounded back nearly upon my head. This silly experiment was never repeated. But the climbing up evening after evening, that was the task of tasks! Ladder after ladder, ladder after ladder, until they seemed interminable, and the top one would never be reached. Panting and perspiring, after stopping again and again, we reached the top at last, where the pure air of heaven fanned our foreheads and filled our lungs with new life, though our flannel dress could not have been wetter if immersed in a river.

My first essay at working underground consisted

in wheeling some of the slabs of mineral from my father's working along a narrow level to the shaft. Here it was upset in what is commonly called a "plot," then filled into the bucket and drawn to the surface. The level was very uneven, so that the barrow, which had a lighted candle stuck in the front end, often slipped from my hands. Some of the corners, too, were very jagged and abrupt, against which I struck my joints, knocking off the skin until the blood ran down. Child as I was I had made up my mind not to cry; but the tears forced themselves out of my eyes upon my face, which I wiped away with my clayey fingers, and tugged and pushed at the heavy barrow. I thought of my mother's smile, the welcome which awaited me at home, and the dear bower of heather where I should watch the moon rise by and by harp in hand; and I struggled on in my mining yoke, chanting quaint couplets of new-made rhyme to the echoes of my cavern. Soon after this I wrote:—

> To-day I've thrashed an old tin-rib,
>   Till I could thrash no more,
> While streams of perspiration ran
>   Unchecked from every pore.
> A fire-cloud drank my spirits up:
>   How longed I for the breeze
> The hoary-headed woodman quaffs
>   Among the forest-trees!

The district in which my boyhood was spent was famous for its harvest of ghost stories. Every large rock and abandoned mine-pit had its white-sheeted spectre. But I set my face against it all, often in the dark nights wandering to the churchyard, and sitting there alone for hours on a grassy grave, in my endeavour to convince my companions of the fallacy of such a belief. My nearest approach to a spectral visitant was in the year 1847. My comrade and I were in Dolcoath mine one night. We had finished our work, and then climbed the ladders to the surface, reaching the top of the shaft as nearly as can be at midnight. We had to take off our underground apparel, and to put on our wearing clothes, which were hanging to iron pins in the blacksmith's shop. The little smithy was silent now, as there was no work done in it except during the day. This shed stood alone, having but one forge, one stack, and one door, opening in halves, in front. Here was a carriage road just wide enough to take a cart, which went on by the end of the shop, until it diverged into another and wider one. Behind the smithy were high heaps of rough rubbish and refuse stones, which had been drawn up from the interior of the mine, and thrown there as useless, entirely barring and blocking up the place, rising almost to a level with the walls of the house. It was difficult indeed for a man to pass over it on foot, much more for a horse and its rider, which seemed impossible.

We entered the blacksmith's shed by the door I have mentioned, which fronted the high road, and had just finished changing our dress, when we heard a tremendous racket outside. We ran to the door, and there was a little horseman on a night-black nag, galloping furiously in front of the smithy. In a moment the horse was checked, and back came the rash rider again, sweeping by like the wind. But instead of continuing on the carriage road, the smoking steed dashed over the heaps of rubbish behind the shed, where a horse had never been known to have gone before. Round, and round, and round the shed it rushed at a frantic pace, each time faster than before, as if the weird animal had wings. I could see no whip in the rider's hand, or bridle-rein—no saddle-stirrup or spur, neither could I discover any face to the horseman. The mystic horse then dashed by us so near that the wind it stirred rushed in our faces. On it went in the very direction of our home, over the road we walked. The smithy stood in a mineral valley known as Bottom Hill, and its sides were very steep, so that it was no easy task to go up them. The carriage road wound along its side, running on a considerable length until it reached the top. There was, however, a footpath for passengers almost in a direct line from the lowest part of the valley to the very edge of the hill. At the distance of every few yards there were flights of steps, so as to surmount it more easily. But a horse to go up that way would be almost like scaling a cliff. What was our surprise, then, when this hazardous horseman, but a few feet in advance of us, dashed right up over these steps! As he leaped from level to level, and from stone to stone, the black horse seemed standing upright on its hind legs. No sound was heard, no crack of whip, no breathing of the jaded beast, but all was still as death.

Of course, the wild horse and its wilder rider reached the high-road on the top of the valley long before we did, though we paced on considerably faster than we were wont. I felt no fear, and hardly expected to see it again, but had resolved that, should it make its appearance, to call out boldly and ask what it wanted. Exactly as we reached the last step of the footpath, which would land us on the main road, there was the black horse and its sooty rider coming full tilt in our faces! I had an opportunity, for a second, to examine the horseman; for by this time the moon had risen, and the light was tolerably good. He seemed as black as ink, armless and legless, and no bigger than a farmer's watchdog. He was bent forward upon the horse's neck, so that he was almost double. I could see no face or features of any kind—no whip, or bridle, or saddle-girth. But down he came sweeping like a storm-wave. We stepped quickly aside, and I shouted "Good night!" but there was no reply, no recognition of our presence, or murmur of any kind. On went the black horse galloping into the midnight—on, on! For several minutes we heard the animal's hoofs rattling and ringing upon the road towards Tuckingmill; and then all was silent, and we saw it no more. What it was I have never discovered to this day—but it was no ghost.

I almost stood alone in this respect among my companions, who were all more or less given to superstition; and I contended, too, that illwishing and overlooking were not in my creed. I had no fear of being thus blighted by the most uncouth man or woman that could be found. To prove this, I went with them to a cottage where an old wizard was staying. It was reported that he had cured the cottager's daughter, who had been unable to walk for some time; but this I greatly doubted.

Her father was so very strong, that it is affirmed he could take his working pony in his arms and lift it over a hedge. The wizard was described as wearing a fustian coat, corduroy trousers, fur-collared waistcoat, hob-nailed boots, with a high hat on his head almost large enough for Giant Bolster, and a tough, crooked gorse stick in his hand. Rumour reported that two days before he had gone to a grave in the neighbourhood, and fixed a wandering ghost in the tomb. But what grieved me more than all was that he carried it on under the guise of religion. To blind the poor people more effectually, he attended meetings, singing hymns and even offering vocal prayer, pretending to follow the Saviour, when he was in close companionship with the father of lies.

I knocked at the door, and we were all admitted; but the bold necromancer was not within. I conversed with the father of the girl, and found he placed implicit confidence in the old wizard, believing him to be a messenger of God who had power over unclean spirits. So far did he go, that he almost made the old hypocrite omnipotent; and when he found that I differed from him, railed upon me with flashing eyes, saying I was like the parson who had called in the morning, and that he supposed I did not believe the Bible. I told him I believed the Bible, every word of it, from beginning to end, but not such an impostor as this wicked old man. "Say you so," he exclaimed, "say you so? Look at this trace of onions hanging against the wall. They belong to him, and if you touch them, and twist them about, you will have your head turned upon your shoulders."

I know he believed what he said, and I determined to try it. I had no fear of any sudden transformation, or of any serious shock to my physical system. Sad that a man who called himself a Christian should believe such an absurdity as this, with the Bible open before him, and the sound of the gospel ringing in his ears. With steady step I advanced towards the trace of onions, and I could see that he was shaking in every limb. His very countenance changed, a great paleness came over it, and he could hardly keep himself seated in his chair. I raised my hands to commit the rash act, he almost fearing to keep his eyes upon me. Had the old wretch himself been there I would have done it without a single pearl of perspiration on my brow. I unshrinkingly grasped the onions one by one, and turned and twisted them in every direction. I am confident that he expected to see my head in some other place, but it still remained upon my shoulders as before. I quietly sat down and confronted him, looking as unperturbed as possible. He was perfectly aghast, and seemed almost afraid to breathe. His eyes singularly glittered as he turned them upon me, and then raised them to the wooden beams over his head.

"You see," said I, " upon what a weak reed you are resting. You have been sadly imposed upon by this man, and misled by the enemy of good. I have defied the enchanter on his own ground, and you see no harm is come of it. None but God can do as you say. Renounce your belief in such vile impositions, and trust in a good Providence, for He has said the very hairs of our head are all numbered." But he was difficult to convince, and bringing his hard hand down upon the deal table with such force as almost to break it, starting to his feet, and looking me full in the face, he roared out, "You have escaped for the present, and only for the present. On your way home an awful catastrophe will overtake you. You are sure to have your head turned upon your shoulders, so as to be looking backwards." I bade him good-bye and proceeded homeward, feeling as easy as if he had forewarned me that I should meet with a shepherd. By this time twilight had come, and a solemn hush had rested upon everything. Stile after stile was passed, cross and cromlech and narrow lane, yet I felt no shock, no twisting of the neck, or turning of the head. I could shut my eyes, open them, turn to the right and left, and gaze on the mystic stars over head. Safe and sound, and altogether untwisted, I reached my father's dwelling, and received my supper from my mother's hands. This incident was not without its moral on the minds of my companions.

Thus the years wore on, and I grew inured to my severe toil. But the Muse never left me above ground or below. I was always courting her, and she was the great solace of my life. In the dust and sulphur of the mine I was making lines to jingle, impelled onward by a strange power I could not resist. I sewed some leaves together and began to copy my effusions. After labouring underground all day, we had to return to our home on the hill, which was about three miles off. My father walked before, and I followed at a short distance behind him; and often the whole journey was traversed without scarcely a word having passed between us. But all this time I was at my rhyming, quietly putting my thoughts together, and writing them in some shady corner of the kitchen on my return. Still I continued to read, borrowing all the books that I possibly could. Captain Jemmy Thomas threw open his library-door to me, and the Rev. Hugh Rogers, the rector of Camborne, lent me Southey's "Remains of Henry Kirke White," which I pondered with great avidity and delight. He afterwards called to see me at my father's house, and read some of my first effusions, which I had just come in from the fields and written with sod-soiled hands; but he gave me no encouragement whatever, rather advising me to discontinue the pursuit of numbers, which was generally the way to poverty and the poorhouse. But this I could not do, though it was kindly spoken, no doubt; for to give up my poetry would fill me with such sorrow as to break my heart. Whenever I met with words I did not understand, I referred to my dictionary, which I bought of a pious blacksmith in the mine, to whom I sometimes recited my pieces, for two half-crowns, wrote them on a slip of paper which I carried in my pocket, and learnt them while I travelled to and from my work. In this way I made a long list of useful syllables my own, which served me ever afterwards. I also paid great attention to any speakers I could depend upon, and thus learnt to pronounce many difficult words, and also to improve my grammar. The Sunday school library in the village helped me greatly. This was my only dictionary, until the late Mrs. Maynard sent me "Ogilvie," in September, 1875.

After a while I began to carry paper and pencil in my pocket, and jot down my rhymes as they came to me. Sometimes I would slip into a field, and write under a hedge so as not to be observed, while my mine-mates walked on and left me. If I found an unfrequented path, I greatly preferred it to the thronged thoroughfare, and went musing on alone, still adding to my poems. I frequently kept my paper and pencil hidden out of sight in my coat-sleeve, held there with the tips of my fingers. This love of solitude made me a little singular, though I was cautious not to give offence. I shunned the crowd then, and I shun the crowd now. I was frequently late on my way to work in the mornings, the simple reason being that then the roads were less crowded, and I had a fairer opportunity for contemplation. Seeing any one behind me who was likely to overtake me, I have slipped into a gap or over a hedge to escape companionship; and though weary to the last degree, I have gone considerably out of my way on my journey homeward, to enjoy the bliss of quiet. From twelve years old until nearly thirty-five, I carried a piece of slate to and from the mine with me in my waistcoat pocket, with a short sharp-pointed nail to scratch down my verses which I contrived to make on the road, that my memory might not be overburdened. Sometimes this was superseded by a stumpy black-lead pencil, and a fragment of paper picked up as I walked along. Poetry was everything, and in all things—the great inspirer, ay, the upholder of my life. I rushed to my verse-making under all circumstances with greater joy than the miser to his hoard, or the school-boy to his evening game among the trees of his father's garden. Weary hands and feet, and body frail with exhaustion, retarded me not; and every sheltered nook and green recess from Stony Lane to Brea River witnessed my rhyming struggle. The day broke and evening deepened, summer and winter refreshed my boyhood and youth, the true tongue of the seasons thrilled me with never-ending themes, and I sang on hopefully, believingly, and undismayed. This was my life-work for the weal of humanity, and by His help I would perform it, renouncing the noisy multitude for silence and the shades. Often have I paced the great carns around my father's dwelling in the musing twilight, until the whispering winds seemed laden with echoes from other spheres, and my rapture has been greater than his who taketh a city. My brothers and sisters increased, and talk became more abundant, so that it was difficult to sit and write amongst them. I therefore stole into the fields and crofts, or sat in the old reedy barn in winter time, scribbling my rustic stanzas with my feet wrapped in my mother's cloak. How have I longed, at such times, for a cell in the castle of Carn Brea, where I thought I could spend a happy existence apart from kith and kin! So enamoured was I of solitude, that my companions were soon left for the shadow of the granite boulders, or the fragrance of the blossoming furze. And in the early spring-time I often walked up and down by the sheltered hedges, where the sun shone, reading and writing. Whether I sat by the kitchen fire with the usual household duties enacting around me; whether I drove the horse in the plough to my father, or wheeled the sod of the meadows into heaps; whether I collected the sheep from the down, or drove the cow to watering, my mind was ever active with my verse-making as the one object of my life. But though the Supreme Giver placed the lyre in my hands, and poetry appeared to be my greatest work in the world, yet I felt that for it I must not neglect my allotted labours, but pursue the path in which Providence had placed me, believing that to act thus would be noble and manly, not depending on literature as a means of pecuniary support, but partaking it as a pleasurable relaxation amid the cares of life. Thus I travelled on through the vale of boyhood, labouring with my hands, and singing with my soul, as solitary as a stranger among my own people, without a single friend to direct me; for how is it possible to educate a poet? What means can you devise to burnish his golden fancies that span the universe like belts of shining jasper? Try, if you please, with the chisel of art; but it will only be a fatal mistake. In the strong words of Joseph Gostick, the only way to educate the poet is to honour him.

About midsummer, when the new stunted grass-tufts were fully developed, I used to be employed in cutting turf on the common, and sometimes bog-peat on the moor. On these occasions my father was generally with me. We sometimes used a flat hoe, and sometimes a small spade, according to the nature of the soil. It was hard work, and so we had to strip to our shirts. My hands were often blistered with the hoe-handle until I could scarcely open them, and my arms seemed ready to drop from my shoulders. Yet I was making rhymes to the swish of the turf-axe and the ring of the shovel, keeping my paper and pencil on the nearest boulder, where the stone-chat would chatter to its wondering brood. My father was a silent man, communing in his work with his Maker, and but little conversation passed between us, so my thoughts had full play; while the heath-scented breezes flowing over the hedgeless down, and kissing the piled-up crags among the mosses, brought to my listening ears the lays of other shores, and the tumble of waters on islands which have never been seen. We two were the only workers on the wide waste, where the view was most extensive, with Druid relics all around us, and the glowing sky with its mystic deeps over our heads. The humming bees had hope-songs on their wings, and the larks in the clear unseen trilled of a sunrise on happier days. I bent to my turf-task with fresher cheerfulness and energy for the music that was in me, and would not have foregone its blessedness to have been clothed in purple and housed in a castle.

My brother William and I slept in one bed in a corner of the great chamber. The rafters and beams were all visible; and often as I lay awake in the moonlight I used to count them, and fancy I saw little horsemen galloping along their edges, or green-coated musicians harping by the curious joints. The wind rushing over the thatch, or thundering in the great chimney, was to me the lyre of wonders intoned by the fingers of mystery. My thoughts would, almost unwooed, resolve themselves into numbers; and as I slept nearest the wall, I often scribbled them upon the plaster, so as to be able to copy them at leisure. And my leisure was very little, much less than that possessed by very many of the same age and station around me; for when disengaged from the mine, my father often kept me in the fields as long as daylight lasted, and sometimes in the barn by candlelight. But I bought up every shred of opportunity, wasting not a single hour, improving every spare moment, hearing the ringing of psalms everywhere. When digging the meadow-ditch, I used to put pencil and paper on the grass a few feet in advance of me, then hoe away, making my poetry at every hack, and when I came up to the sheet write down my verses. And though thus diligent in the pursuit of poetry from boyhood until the keepers of the house are beginning to tremble, I can conscientiously affirm that I have not neglected for it one single social duty. From first to last the majority of my poems have been written in the open air—in lanes and leas, by old stiles and farm-gates, rocks, and rivers, and mossy moors. When about thirteen or fourteen, I purchased a small fife for a few pence, on which I learnt to play several tunes. But the most interesting feature in connection with it was, perhaps, my sitting alone among the furze-bushes and thyme-banks fifing my verses into existence. After playing them over and over again,

I wrote them down on paper with my well-worn pencil, and at leisure transferred them to my scrap-book. All my published volumes, tracts, pamphlets, periodical articles, and letters, have been copied or written whilst sitting up in my chair, holding the sheet in my hand.

I have never been guilty of writing but two satirical poems, and both of these I destroyed. The first was on a young schoolmaster who was connected with our village Institute. He delivered a lecture to the class on Phrenology, which I made a theme for versifying, censuring the subject much more than the speaker. I read my production to a few of the neighbours, which came to the lecturer's ears, and he visited me in my father's house on the hill, saying he had heard I had penned some singular stanzas concerning his address, and asking me if I would read them in his hearing? I produced them from the drawer where I kept my jingles, and read them to him by the farm-yard gate. It made him rather angry, and he said it was a great deal worse than he could have imagined, and it would be hard for him to forgive me unless I tore the manuscript in pieces before his eyes. I twitched it into shreds, and scattered it hither and thither to the mountain-winds, he earnestly looking on all the time. We parted in peace; and I never had another copy. The second satire was on a stupid dentist, who had the hardihood to jerk out two of my teeth at a twitch, and one of them quite sound. This poem I lent to a valued Friend at Camborne; and when he returned it to me, he very wisely said, "John Harris, I advise thee to put that piece in between the bars of the grate." I acted on his advice; and that effusion, too, was lost for ever. Thus suddenly and wisely ended my composition of satire.

CHAPTER III.

HOME LIFE.

I CANNOT forget when I first read Campbell's "Gertrude of Wyoming." I was then in my teens, with a thirst for poetry, which could not be quenched. I had selected it from the library in the village school, and, pocketing my treasure, hastened to a secluded place where I might peruse it in quiet. It was a little fern-covered hollow on the side of a lovely dell. Here I threw myself down, and drew the book from my pocket. At my feet a clear stream went wandering on its way; birds sang on the branches of the trees over my head; sweet flowers shed a delicious fragrance around; bees hummed, and butterflies floated among the honied cups; while before me, as through a silver vista, rose the sun-lighted hills of the Land's End, and the blue waters of the Atlantic Ocean. On I read, wading deeper and deeper in liquid beauty, bound to the charming story by a great spell; and when at last I closed the volume, and started up to climb the hill where my parents resided, I felt soul-full with the lore of the Muses.

Soon after this, from the same library, I was gladdened with the loan of that marvellous book —Pollok's "Course of Time." I carried it with me wherever I went, when I was not in the mine; and the grand thoughts therein contained followed me like living forms, or echoes from the heights of Carmel. No book stirred my soul deeper than this; and I felt thankful that such a man had ever existed to sweep the sacred lyre. By brooks and streams it was my choice companion, and where the rude rocks taught me on my own wild fens. From that time until the present period it has been a comfort and a joy, though I did not possess a copy of my own until ten years ago which was presented to me by the late Mr. John Little, of London. I have often placed it under my pillow at night; and I used to think I should like to sleep with it in my coffin.

The first poetical composition which I prepared for the press was a polemical dialogue between a workman and his master. This was written soon after a strike for wages among some of the dissatisfied miners in a portion of my own district. I well remember how the manufacturing of this dialogue hurried sleep from my eyes for a whole night; and when at last it was finished, I copied it upon several sheets of clean white paper, and took it to a printer at Camborne, who, after keeping it a long time, returned it with these ominous words, "I do not think it is worth printing." I know now he was quite right. Imagine my horror, however, on hearing this crushing speech, and the sadness of my soul as I climbed the old mountain to my mother's dwelling. Suffice it to say that I destroyed my poem, and never more indulged in this species of jingling ware.

Our old red horse, Golly, had, I think, much more knowledge than his compeers. When I drove him in the plough, he looked at me so eagerly as if he knew I was writing verses to the regularity of his tread. When I mounted his back, and rode him to watering on the downs, he kept on so steadily as if he knew there was a juvenile jingler astride his glossy coat. When I held him in the paddock, he gathered his mouthfuls so deliberately, and munched the grasses so contentedly, as if he were aware that a new poem was concocting in his presence to gladden the wondering world. In the wain, or the harrow, or the roller, he acted so judiciously as if he were conscious that a tiny peasant-piper was at his side. But when we went to Connor Bar for sand in the newly-painted cart, how he jogged away through long long miles of narrow lanes, where the birds sang on the bushes, and the gossamer hung in the brakes, needing not a single chirrup, or gee ho, or crack of whip, as if his genuine instinct revealed to him that a mountain-bred muser was writing poetry to the sound of his hoofs. And so I was, while the trailing vetch and honeysuckle whispered from the hedges. He had a snug little stable in a corner of one of our meadows, and in the stable a manger which was a model of its kind. I used to take his hay and oaten straw to him from the old barn; and even now I seem to see his great eyes blinking upon me as I opened the door, and to hear his cheerful neigh, which, interpreted, seemed to be, "Thank you very much for bringing me my sweet provender." Our farm being a somewhat stony one, thistles were sometimes found amongst the hay. If Golly discovered one of those prickly customers in the armful I chanced to bring him, he would never stop pushing his great nose until he thrust it clear out of the manger: and then he would gather up the sweet grass in delicious mouthfuls, chewing diligently away until he had finished his repast, the most contented old horse that ever was seen. Thus he taught me a truthful lesson. Dear, defunct old Golly! it is pleasant, even now, to recall his memory, though his bones have long mouldered into dust, and the fields and lanes which once knew him know him no more. The rhythm of many a newborn lyric has been murmured in his ears.

One lovely Sabbath morning I was sitting amid the heather of my bower, listening to the lark overhead, and the murmuring brooklet in the adjoining moor. I was on my way to school, and only turned aside here for the joy it gave me. Stalking up the croft were two young men, almost our nearest neighbours, who were not over-scrupulous in their morals. This I knew, and had sometimes suffered from their taunts. They persuaded me with all their cunning to break the Sabbath, and absent myself from my class; but this conscience would not allow me to do. I thought of the grief of my father and mother, were I to consent to sin, but more than all of Him who had been the guide of my youth. I went to my little chapel, and they to their unholy pursuits. Soon after this they endeavoured to draw me into disreputable company; but, seeing my danger, I mercifully escaped. Once out of the net, I praised God among the gorse-bushes and rocks on my way homeward with streaming eyes; and I tremble even now when I think, had I yielded, what the consequences might have been. But I was kept by His power who watches the fall of the sparrow. These two hardened transgressors emigrated to the wilds of the West; and in the middle of a mighty forest, with no one near them but a lonely traveller, they were suddenly smitten with a fatal disease, dying in darkness in the midst of the vast solitude. They were both buried in one rude grave, without tear or funeral-rite, which is now lost in the boundless wilderness; and the wild beasts prowl over their nameless tomb. A descriptive passage relating to this painful event is found in my Wayside Pictures.

The first essay of mine ever steeped in printer's ink was a dirge on the death of some miners who were accidently killed in Carn Brea. These verses were given to a poor blind man; and I remember with what intense joy I listened in the crowd as he sang them up and down the market at Camborne.

SHUNNING THE BEER HOUSE.

"An Address to the Robin" came next, in one of the Wesleyan magazines, which was followed by "The First Primrose," and "The Story of Robin Redbreast." The two latter pieces were much praised by the editor, which encouraged me to go on. A tailor at Camborne now lent me Robert Bloomfield; and the zest with which I perused it, it is impossible to portray. I began to save my pence; and the first books I bought were a Bible and a hymn-book, and then Shakespere. My evenings were devoted to study, chiefly out of doors, wandering about the wilds with a book in my pocket, or my pencil and paper in my hand. Nothing could discourage me or divert me from my purpose. If my fingers tingled with cold, I rubbed my hands together, or beat them on my shoulders, as I had seen my father do in the fields. If my feet ached and felt benumbed, I ran along the sheep-paths, or scampered over the moss on the lee side of the hedge, until relief came, and the blood coursed freely through my veins. This was done in my hours of leisure, which many around me worse than wasted. Once only I entered a beer-house alone with the intent of drinking. Many youths of my own age and occupation were sitting there, smoking and chatting over their cups. I looked around me for a few minutes, and concluded that if I continued to visit the alehouse I should grow up like these people, and not advance one single step beyond by present position. My resolve was quickly made, that, with the help of Him whom I desire to serve, I would never alone enter such a place again—and I never did. Summers and winters passed by, I struggled on in rain and sunshine, cold and heat, the love of books increasing more and more, the enkindled passion for poetry burning in my breast, which all the heavy hardships of my lot could not suppress, keeping my back perpetually on the beer-house door. Were there days of rain and storm, or drizzling mist, which are often, as holidays, weariness and misery to many? They were gilt with glory for me; for in some "cell confined" I was then at my song-grinding as happy as a monarch, while visions of unuttered beauty crowded upon my soul.

Thus year was added to year with no abatement in my daily toil or in my pursuance of poetry, until love found me in the fields, and I became the grateful possessor of my good wife Jane. I was then twenty-five, and up to twenty-three had carried all my earnings to my mother. Our first place of residence was a two-roomed dwelling in the village of Troon. I was then a tributer in the mine; and for the first ten months of our married life fortune was against me, so that my earnings amounted to no more than ten-pence a day. How we contrived to exist on this small pittance without going into debt, I cannot tell; yet so it was. Then the tide turned, mineral was discovered, Providence blest my labours, and I soon became the owner of two hundred pounds. With a portion of this sum I built a house at Troon-Moor by the river, where we lived happily for many years. In the erection of this dwelling I worked labouriously. Following my stated duties in the mine, I gave every hour of leisure, for two summers and winters, in procuring material for its walls. Evenings and mornings I was in the quarry, and sometimes by moonlight, raising and conveying stone to the site of the building. Often under the scorching sun my shirt and flannel have been as wet with perspiration as if immersed in water. I have frequently worked all night in the mine, and half the next day at my new house, thus robbing nature of its required rest. But I did it cheerfully, and often with a glad song upon my lips, with the hope of procuring a humble home for my wife and children. My father allowed me to have his horse and cart; and old Golly and I had many a rough pull and shove before the work was over. Even in the midst of this harsh toil I heard rills of tenderest music, and wrote rhymes in my shirt-sleeves, sitting on the shafts of the empty cart, or following the full load paper in hand. My brother William assisted me in cutting the granite in our croft on Bolennowe Carne, when we used drills and iron wedges. These heavy pieces of stone were all carted from the downs, at a distance of more than a mile, I always driving the horse myself. Thus with incredible labour I accomplished it all, raising and carrying every stone and every shovelful of clay in the building, and also in the walls of the garden, doing it in odd hours when too many of my own calling were idly smoking their pipes with their hands in their pockets, or drinking away their time and money in the public house. It amazes me even now to think of my perseverance; nor did I rest until the last stone was laid, the roof put on, and the little cottage was our own. With thankful hearts we entered it: and here I wrote my " Love of Home," and "Kynance Cove." Here, too, our second child was born and passed away, and tears of anguish fell on our first gathered flower. Every stone cost me a drop of sweat, and every clod of clay a fresh respiration; so no wonder that I loved it, writing peace upon its walls.

Still I had no study, no room to call my own, where I might sit in quiet with my books and the Muses. How much I longed for it I cannot tell, or how many tears I shed. In hours of leisure, on holidays, and intervals of release from the drudgery of the mine, I often had recourse to my old haunts on the hill, writing my poems among the rocks, in sheltered corners where the mosses were plentiful, by gorse-bushes fragrant with yellow flowers, or in the shallow mine-pits over-hung with brambles and heather. Here I remained in blissful meditation, far away from the busy multitude, sometimes writing on the crown of my hat, the bar of an old gate, or the face of a lichened boulder, while the mystery of the mighty moors filled my fancy, and the larks soared and sang in the blue ether. A study of four walls might not, after all, have been more propitious.

Soon after our marriage, the Rev. G. T. Bull, of Treslothan, seeing I was fond of poetry, lent me a volume of Shakespere. The first play I read was "Romeo and Juliet," which I greedily devoured travelling over a wide downs near my father's house. The delight I experienced is beyond words to describe, as the sun sank behind the western waters, and the purple clouds of evening fringed the horizon. The bitters of life changed to sweetness in my cup, and the wilderness around me was a region of fairies. Sometimes I cried, sometimes I shouted for joy; and over the genii-peopled heights a new world burst upon my view. Admitted into the palace of enchantment, I passed the gateway again and again, and heard music and saw visions of ethereal loveliness which filled me with a fuller existence. In the lovely home of the Misses Thomas I first heard Mr. Bull read some choice extracts from Byron's "Childe Harold." The masterly might of this powerful magician held me entranced. For weeks and months I could hear or think of nothing else. To borrow the book and read it for myself, what a treat! but nobody would think of lending it to me. A short time afterwards, Mr. Charles Rule, who was kind to me when a lad in the mine, invited me to his house. I went, was ushered into the drawing room, and seeing several books upon the table, concluded that the nearest by me must surely be "Childe Harold." I timidly put forth my hand and took it; but was a little surprised to find that it was a New Testament.

My love for Burns has already been mentioned, which did not grow less as age increased. The truth waxes brighter in the flight of years; and true song ever retains its genuine ring. My younger brother James possessed an eighteenpenny copy of Burns's Poems, to which I had access: but on my removal to Falmouth, Mr. Michael Little presented me with a large illustrated and complete edition of his works. One day, as a relaxation, I was reading Burns in our Troon-Moor home. No one can tell the ecstasy of my spirit, or the deep joy of my heart. Not only was I tired with my mine-work, but also crippled in the quarry raising stone for the garden-wall. I believe I was in my shirt-sleeves, when a middle-aged matron entered my home who was looked upon as one of the most respectable inhabitants of the neighbourhood. Seeing a small book before me, she asked what it was. I told her; and her answer surely displayed her prejudice and her narrowness of mind. Looking at me with severity in her features, she exclaimed, "You ought to be ashamed of yourself! You, a local preacher, and reading Burns!" This strange sin placed me quite beyond the reach of her favours, and I do not remember her ever speaking to me afterwards. But no strictures of hers could induce me to shut up this fountain of pure melody.

For more than twenty years I was an underground miner, toiling in the depths of Dolcoath. Here I laboured from morning till night, and often from night till morning, frequently in sulphur and dust almost to suffocation. Sometimes I stood in slime and water above my knees, and then in levels so badly ventilated that the very stones were hot, and the rarefied air caused the perspiration to stream into my boots in rills, though I doffed my flannel shirt and worked naked to the waist. Sometimes I stood on a stage hung in ropes in the middle of a wide working, where my life depended on a single nail driven into a plank. Had the nail slipped, I should have been pitched headlong on the broken rocks more than twenty feet below. Sometimes I stood on a narrow board high up in some dark working, holding the drill, or smiting it with the mallet, smeared all over with mineral, so that my nearest friends would hardly know me, until my bones ached with the severity of my task, and the blood dropped off my elbows. Sometimes I had to dig through the ground where it was impossible to stand upright, and sometimes to work all day as if clinging to the face of a cliff. Sometimes I have been so exhausted as to lie down and sleep on the sharp flints, and sometimes so thirsty that I have drunk stale water from the keg, closing my teeth to keep back the worms. Sometimes I had wages to receive at the end of the month, and sometimes I had none. But I despaired not, nor turned the nymph of Song from my side. She murmured among the tinctured slabs, cheered me in the hot air of the closest cell, when panting under the mallet or the sledge, the pick or the levering-bar, wheeling the barrow, pushing the waggon, filling the bucket, or lifting the severed stones, bringing down into the dense darkness the scent of flowers, green leaves and clover meadows, whilst the lark's shrill carol rang in my soul. My verses have been written on smooth pieces of house-slate, roof-tile, iron wedges underground, and even on my thumb-nails, the principal delineations being those of my own county.

In this way the angel of music strove to cheat the tyranny of labour, and kept me company in the gloom. "Take care of yourself," said one of the mine-agents when I was very weak and poorly, and left me breaking rocks in the powder-smoke with an enormous sledge that I could scarcely lift higher than my chin. It was pleasant, on one occasion, to be called into the account-house at Dolcoath, and to be presented by the agents with half-a-sovereign, for my "sobriety and good conduct." After the fatigue of the day below, when my bones ached and my heart was heavy, I had to climb the long ladders, one after another, to reach the surface of the earth and home; for this was before the man-engine was adopted, a laudable invention for the comfort of miners by the late Charles Fox, Esq. By this time I was often so weary that I could scarcely drag myself along. It was full two miles to my house; and in the winter season it was frequently rain, through which I had to trudge without cape or overcoat, so that by the time I reached my dwelling I was wet to the skin. Ye who have pictured parlours, and well-filled libraries, with every other accessory to study, may well ask what spirit I had for reading and writing then? Though my hands were hardened with the tool-handle, and scarred with the callous flints, nothing could daunt the desire within me, or suppress the longings of my soul; and every moment of leisure was devoted to the one object I had in view. Often have I rocked my children in the cradle, and hummed my song into existence at the same time, which helped to lull the little ones to sleep. Whilst their mother has been working about the house, I have held them on my knees and wrote my verses with their ringing prattle in my ears. No man was happier than I when I led them forth into the fields and crofts, among the gentle rivulets and high rocks, they to gather ferns and flowers, and I to write because my heart was full. One of these scenes perpetually haunts me. We had climbed a rushy hillock, and near its summit sat in the sun. Below us was a clear river shining and tumbling over the pebbles; behind us, and on each side, was the wide moorland stretching away wider and yet wider still; a few thatched cottages were scattered here and there, from the open doors of which snatches of household song floated up to us in our green bower; whilst over head the great mysterious sky spread out its magnificence. A daughter sat on each side of me: and in deep silence we watched this glowing scene.

Thus my children became my companions. They were never happier than when with me, nor I than when with them. They were with me when I wrote my "War-Fiend" at the head of the Reens, under the young fir-trees by the brook. They knew when I was thoughtful, and seldom disturbed me, playing about the banks till I rose to go. They shared in our humbleness, content with what Providence sent us, filling our wayside home with light, and gladdening our hearts more than the clink of silver, or the glitter of gold. All day long I struggled and strove far below the sound of the river, or the sight of the sun; yet the remembrance of their dear faces cheered me in the conflict, and I shook off the bands of lassitude and hastened to meet them with sunshine in my soul. And when any little unexpected comfort came, how my heart throbbed to meet them at the hearth, that we might share it together, and my bliss was surely then a shadow of that which angels feel in heaven. In adverse times, too, when my month's earnings would scarcely purchase bread, on its receipt I have walked sadly through the fields and lanes, wiping off the tears because I could not afford to purchase anything nice for my children. On such oppressive seasons I have often filled my outside pocket with blackberries from the hedges, that they might not be altogether disappointed. They would watch for me through the window as I came up the garden, lifting their hands, their bright eyes shining with delight; and the possession of the wild berries of the brake filled them with the greatest joy. I felt I was poor no longer, and wiped my eyes in thankfulness, even as I wipe them now; and we sallied forth to seek for poems among the bushes.

This incident called forth the following simple verses, which were first published with my "Kynance Cove," in 1858.

> Come to me, smiling little ones,
>   And prattle in my ear;
> Don't let it fright you from your sire,
>   This big, round, falling tear.
> It came into your father's eye,
>   When coming home to you,
> Although the earth was beautiful,
>   The far-off sky was blue.
>
> You ask me why it gushes forth,
>   This sorrow-speaking tear:
> In hastening home, sweet cherub ones,
>   My thoughts were with you here.
> Glad harvest songs were floating round
>   Beneath the summer sky:
> In spite of Nature's minstrelsy,
>   The tears came in my eye.
>
> You wonder still why it could be,
>   At such a merry time,
> When little robin's song rose o'er
>   The happy reapers' chime.

And you were promised such rare things
  When I came home to you,—
Long dainty rods of sugar-stick,
  And picture rhyme-books too.

So you've been waiting all this time
  Within my lowly cot,
And gazing through the casement cried
  "He's coming, is he not?"
Ye run with looks of winning love
  No heart can e'er withstand,
With lips that prattle innocence,
  And open outstretched hand.

I'll tell you why the tear appeared,
  When travelling o'er the mead;
Tis pay-day, and my hard-earned hire
  Was very small indeed:
No! not enough to purchase food,
  In this dark day of dearth,
For you, my shining olive leaves,
  That gem my household hearth.

Ah! when this pittance I received,
  None but our Father knows,
How my first thoughts flew home to you;
  Twas then the tear uprose.
So through the market town I passed,
  Nor anything I had,
No, not a sugar-kiss for you,
  I felt so very sad.

I plucked those berries from the bush,
  In coming o'er the lea;
And here they are, my little loves,
  As ripe as ripe can be.
Ye eat them up so heartily,
  And seemed so pleased and gay,
I'll smile again, my babes, with you,
  And dash the tear away.

Come, we will sit us down once more,
  And sing the song you love,
Of little Jane, your humming sire,
  And her the mother dove.
I have no mines of sparkling ore,
  No diamonds of rich dye;
But ye are gems I value more
  Than all beneath the sky.

And since ye cheer my hours of gloom,
  And hours of sunshine too,
I'll clasp ye closer to my heart,
  And thank the Lord for you.
Blest be the Hand that placed you here,
  Upon my humble floor:
I'll trust His Providence to feed
  The flowerets of the moor.

In a more recent effusion, written in 1880, called "The Faces at the Pane," and published in my last work, I have again revived it:—

Where'er I go, whate'er I do,
  A vision meets mine eye,
From the far valleys of the past,
  Flecked with the summer sky.
It comes in days of quiet trust,
  It comes in wind and rain,
It comes when harvest crowns the earth,—
  The faces at the pane.

When toiling in the darksome mine,
  As tired as tired could be,
How has the glad thought cheered my soul,
  My children watch for me!
And as I oped the garden gate,
  Which led into the lane,
How danced my heart to see once more
  The faces at the pane!

Two little girls with gleaming eyes,
   With soft and shining hair,
And sweetest prattle on their lips,
   Were watching for me there.
One in the grave is sleeping now,
   And one has crossed the main;
Yet still I see, where'er I be,
   The faces at the pane.

And when I brought some hedgerow fruit,
   Or darling hedgerow flowers,
Which they were early taught to love,
   Their kisses came in showers.
O, precious were those distant days,
   Which may not come again,
Made brighter, fairer, fresher for
   The faces at the pane.

Old age has bound me in its bands,
   And o'er the solemn sea
I seem to hear mysterious sounds
   From unknown lake and lea.
But through the cares that lie behind,
   Along the murky plain,
I see as if but yesterday
   The faces at the pane.

Few retrospects have greater joy,
   Now life is waning fast,
And fewer visions sun my soul
   Like this from out the past.
And thank I Him who giveth much
   Our gratitude to gain,
Nor least among His greater gifts
   The faces at the pane.

We were at supper one evening in Troon-Moor house, our two daughters in the window, I at the end of the kitchen table, and Jane sitting on a chair beside it. We had fried onions, and the flavour was very agreeable. I was hungry, having just returned from a long day's labour in the mine. Suddenly we heard a step in the garden, and then a knock at the door. My wife opened it, and I heard a gruff voice say, "Does the young Milton live here?" My wife asked the possessor of the gruff voice to walk in; and we soon discovered that it was the Rev. G. Collins. We invited him to partake of our meal, to which he at once assented, eating the onions with a spoon, exclaiming almost at every mouthful, "I like these fried leeks." He asked for my latest production, and I gave him "The Child's First Prayer," in MS. He quietly read it; and before he had finished I could see the tears running down his face. Besides the two daughters, Jane and Lucretia, already named, we were afterwards blest with two sons, Howard and Alfred.

Shall we take a peep, dear reader, at my Troon-Moor home? I have just returned from the hard drudgery of my daily toil in the interior of the mine, exhausted and cruelly crushed. A few worn books are piled up in a corner on some narrow shelves, three of the most conspicuous being, Walker's Dictionary, sweet Burns, and Shakespere. Nor must I forget my Bible, the gift of my sainted father, the sweet stories of which so charmed me when a boy. Scraps of paper, written over with jingling rhyme, lie among the volumes, and sleep in quiet nooks, jotted by my own hand. A small fire is burning in the stove; on one side of it sits my industrious wife, plying her needle with a smile upon her face; a bright girl, with soft poetic eyes, is conning her lessons at my feet, and a blue-eyed boy, like a laughing Cupid, is climbing my knees and kissing my pale brow. Crushed and crippled with the labours of the day, I let fall a tear upon the cheek of my little one, return his sweet caress, and for a season forget my lassitude as I gaze into the fire, where a thousand strange shapes flit to and fro. I share my frugal meal with my dear ones, and bless God for what they enjoy. Now I tell the children their wonted story, join them in their sports, dance baby in my arms, or write my poetry as they crow upon my knees. How sweet is my domestic bliss! and bright angels are bending over the walls of glory to gaze upon the scene. And when my cottage-roses fall asleep, and fold themselves in beauty, and quiet is brooding over all, it is then that the principal portion of my verses will be written, and my thoughts twined into rhyme.

Through the appearance of my "First Primrose" in the Magazine, Doctor George Smith, of Camborne, came to know me, and kindly invited me to his house at Trevu. After one or two calls, I told him I should like to make an attempt at publishing, but I scarcely knew how to begin. The Doctor paced his room, and after a few turns said, "John, copy some of your best pieces, and I will submit them to my friends, and see what they will say about it." This was done, and I anxiously waited to hear the verdict of my judges. I have now forgotten all the others, except that of Doctor Etheridge, who was a genuine classical scholar and a poet. He wrote to my patron to say, "I would recommend 'The Love of Home,' and 'My Mother's Voice,' to the world. Encourage the author, and he will take his stand among the English poets." This was sufficient, and I was persuaded to collect pieces enough together to make an eighteen-penny volume, which I dedicated to Doctor Smith, he acting for me with my printer. This was in the year 1853. The Doctor prepared a written prospectus for me, and several of the gentry in the neighbourhood subscribed to the work; one of my best friends being Mr. John Budge, who pronounced my sonnet to the lark to be equal to Wordsworth. The book was entitled "Lays from the Mine, the Moor, and the Mountain." It was well received by the public and the press, and was followed by a second and an enlarged edition in about eighteen months. It was then that a friendship was first formed between me and Dr. J. A. Langford, of Birmingham, which continues to this day. He visited us in 1872, and was deeply interested in Mr. Joshua Fox and the birds. Captain Charles Thomas, the managing agent of the mine where I worked, told me that he was so pleased with my poems that he remained out of bed nearly the whole of one night reading them. He also strove to help me, by showing the book to one of the richest adventurers in the mine, who gained his thousands a year through the excessive toil of the poor men. It was told me afterwards that he took up the volume, turned it round, flung it upon the account-house table, and exclaimed, "Let him work on, let him work on," wounding me to tears. He refused to subscribe for a single copy. How I persevered amid such rough labour and such strange rebuffs seems now almost incredible. But nothing could turn me from my purpose, or wrest the Muse from my embrace.

By this time a large number of pieces were treasured up in my drawer, the surplus of a heap which my wife and I burnt in an unused fireplace upstairs. How carefully I guarded my manuscripts none but a poor poet can tell. Mr. Henry Gill, of Tiverton, sent me a pound, with which my wife and I visited the Land's End, travelling on foot from Penzance to the Logan Rock, and from thence to the "First and Last" in one day. This journey resulted in my poem, "The Land's End." How I revelled in the fresh air, the sounds and sights of this well-known promontory, none but those who have escaped from the sulphur of the mine, or the dust of the factory, can understand. My first impressions of the Land's End are thus recorded in a communication to Edward Bastin, August 28, 1856.

Well, here we are in a fog-shroud, groping our way around the Logan Rock, and shivering amidst the grandeur of the Land's End: mist, mist, nothing but mist! I declare I was quite angry with the fog-sprite; for, from the first moment we entered on this wild array of crags, to the time I am now pencilling these lines in the "First and Last," this invisible tormentor has been sputtering away till we are quite drenched through to the skin. The Land's End is the most sublime thing I have yet seen in nature. How the dark waves dash against those rocks, and foam and hiss, moaning hoarse tales of storms, and shipwrecks, and callous wreckers in days of old! Everlastingly they come and go, smiting the walls of the old cliff with giant fury, and then recoiling in jets of foam! The light-house in the midst of the waters, and the sea-birds on the ledges of the rocks, or floating over the waves, or chiming to the hoarse bass of the billows, as they dash through the sparry grottoes,—all conspire to endear it to the memory. The mist is still falling, or rather driving. We are hastening back over the moor, fragrant with flowers, to our nest for the night, ever and anon pulling off a tuft of heather, and asking questions of our cheerful guide, who seems to tell us all he knows. And now the old clock on the top of the stairs is striking eight, Jane is almost exhausted with the day's long journey, and for the *first time in my life* I retire to rest away from home.

The old clock struck ten, eleven, and still I slept not. The little white chamber seemed full of wicked elves, which prided themselves on keeping my eyelids open. The moan of the old ocean came up on the blast, which hurried over the house-top with a furious twitch; and a couple of fat travellers in an adjoining room kept whistling and singing, so that I wished them somewhere else. I never expected to get into dream-land or sleep-land, and was just about to leap out of bed, and commence an angry poem, or rush down to the wild beach and listen to the midnight songs of the sea, when sweet sleep fell on me like a beautiful spell. When I awoke, the winds were hushed, the mist was gone, the light of the morning was streaming through the window, the sea-birds were wheeling over the down, a robin sang under the eaves of the old inn, and the lighthouse was shining like an angel in the midst of the waters. So away we went in the matin breezes, down, down past Johnson's Head, away on the extreme crags of the Land's End; and, O, what a wilderness of wonders was there! We felt doubly paid for the mist, doubly paid for our long walk, as the huge clouds rolled back from the rising sun, and the great sea became bluer and bluer, and the Scilly Islands rose up to view, and the noisy gulls called to each other in the crevices of the cliff, or cried upon the waters like poets of the billows. I stood upon one of the crags and repeated Charles Wesley's hymn, and felt I had begun a new era in my existence. The Land's End is like a great craggy poem, epic or otherwise. Every poet should read it, and make it his own.

Serious longings now came over me to be released from underground darkness, and to be employed in some humble sphere above ground. But months and months passed, with all the drag and drudgery consequent on a miner's life, and I was still chained by circumstances to the rock. The pure air was what I sighed for, and the inspiration of Nature and man. Not that I was discontented with my lot where Providence had placed me; but would not some vocation where I might sometimes see the blue sky, the fields and flowers, and hear the wild birds and the rushing rivers, conduce greatly to my already failing health, and be more propitious to my poetry? I prayed about it in the mine-caves, and in the narrow lanes going to and coming from my work. Nor can I forget a beautiful summer evening, when the purple light was resting on tree-top and tower, and the wings of angels seemed fluttering in the firs, how I wandered down the valley by a clear stream, with tears upon my face and a prayer upon my lips, that, if it were His will, I might speedily be delivered from the dungeon in which I pined. The power of the Almighty seemed resting on the heights, and the hemisphere was full of His presence. I saw I was selfish, and felt willing to submit to His will. If the mine must be my grave, so let it be; or if taken out of it, it was well. I would patiently and cheerfully submit; and soon relief came.

CHAPTER IV.

BOOK MAKING.

THROUGHOUT my mining-life I have had several narrow escapes from sudden death. Once when at the bottom of the mine, the bucket-chain suddenly severed, and came roaring down the shaft with rocks and rubbish. I and my comrade had scarcely time to escape; and one of the smaller fragments of stone cut open my forehead, leaving a visible scar to this day. Then the man-engine accidentally broke, hurling twenty men headlong into the pit, and I amongst them. A few scars and bruises were my only injuries. Standing before a tin-stope on the smallest foothold, a thin piece of flint, air-impelled, struck me on the face, cutting my lips and breaking some of my front teeth. Had I fallen backwards among the huge slabs, death must have been instantaneous. Passing over a narrow plank, a hole exploded at my feet, throwing a shower of stones around me; but not a single hair of my head was injured. A more wonderful interposition of Divine Providence may be traced, perhaps, in the following record. Our party consisted of five men working in a sink. Two of them were my younger brothers. Over our heads the ground was expended; and there was a huge cavern higher and farther than the light of the candle would reveal. Here hung huge rocks as if by hairs, and we knew it not. We were all teachers in a Sunday school, and on the tea and cake anniversary remained out of our working to attend the festival. Some men who laboured near us, at the time when we were in the green field singing hymns and thanking God, heard a fearful crash in our working, and on hastening to see what it was, found the place quite full of flinty rocks. They had suddenly fallen from above, exactly in the place where we should have been, and would have crushed us to powder were it not for the Sunday school treat.

Another incident is fresh in my memory. Uncle Will and I were working together underground, digging in a singularly narrow place after copper ore. It was a very unfrequented part of the mine, where the sound of another labourer's hammer was not heard on the rock. Uncle Will was an old man, and so I let him sit upon a board a little way behind the working, charging him to take care and keep his light burning, whilst I used the pick and iron wedges in cutting through the lode. Nearly half-an-hour, perhaps, had thus passed, and not a word had been spoken between us, when, by some mischance, I happened to strike the candle which was giving me light in the working, and which was stuck to a fragment of the rock with soft clay, called Saint Ann's, with the point of the pick, knocking it among the rubbish, so that it was extinguished immediately. Looking back on Uncle Will, I was perfectly astounded to find that his candle, too, was gone out, with the exception of a spark of fire in the wick, at which the old man was blowing with all his might, endeavouring in vain to enkindle it. A puff or two more, and we were in utter darkness. I questioned my unwatchful comrade about it, and his reply was, "O, dear! I caught a nod, and awoke just in time to see my candle falling."

And now what could we do? To cry for help would be utterly useless; as well might the wrecked mariner, floating on a board, call to the moon. To sound the rock, and give the understood signal with miners, would also be fruitless, as we were too isolated for anything of this sort. Nor had we any means to strike a light, for this occurred before lucifer matches had been invented. If we remained there, it might be many days before any help reached us, and in that time we should suffer much from hunger and thirst, to say nothing of cold, and perhaps die of starvation. Seeing our position thus critically extreme, I addressed Uncle Will, saying there was no other course for us than to endeavour to grope our way through the great darkness to the top of the mine. It was a serious undertaking, but the only way likely at all to prove effectual. Better run this risk than sit there to die in the sickly, sulphurous cell. Should we try? And Uncle Will answered, "Yes."

Taking a pick in my hand to feel the way, I went before, and Uncle Will followed after. How slowly we advanced! Sometimes we had to ascend the face of the rock, where little notches were cut for our feet, the omission of one of which would be swift destruction. Sometimes we had a ladder to climb, and land upon the narrowest platform, full of holes, where a slip of the foot would be our ruin. Sometimes we had low workings to crawl through, where we could not stand upright, and flinty rocks to scramble over with teeth as sharp as swords. Then we had long levels to pass through, in which were deep sinks, with only a single narrow plank across them, which warped and bent as we came upon it, crawling over on our hands and knees. I often had to cheer Uncle Will with words of encouragement, bidding him to keep directly behind me, while I had to feel my way inch by inch, and foot by foot, with the pick-handle. Now we had a set of ladders to mount, shifting this way and that way as we reached the top of one to gain the foot of the other, the ascent being no wider than an ordinary well.

Slowly, silently, and solemnly we went; and in the pauses of our steps we could hear the beating of our heart against our side. A single slip of the foot, and we should be lost in some grim excavation where we might be undiscovered until the sea gave up its dead, and the earth put on her flaming funeral-shroud. Whenever we could, we felt the rock at our side, or under our feet, and toiled on. But now we had to pass by a shaft, where the footway was not more than three feet wide, which yawned under us some two hundred fathoms deep. There was no chain, or rope, or railing around it, or security of any kind. It was useless to strain our eyes to try to catch a gleam of light; we might as well have kept them closed, for the great gloom was as perfect as that in the house of the dead. This shaft was the most dangerous part of the way; and I cannot tell you how slowly we passed it. Sometimes a loose stone, disturbed by our movements, would roll into the void, and go sounding down the dreadful depths, until we could hear it no longer. Thus we stole onward, with the thought of home, wife, and children in our minds. Could we cross this cruel gulf, hope would revive, for then the ladders would almost be in a direct perpendicular line to the top. At last we got over, and Uncle Will and his guide were again ascending. We felt now comparatively safe. This was the regularly-used way up and down the mine, and we might, perhaps, soon meet some one with a light; and if not, we felt almost certain of reaching the top. Up we go, up, up; ladder after ladder, ladder after ladder, each round bringing us nearer to liberty and home. By and bye, when looking upward, we saw a speck of light like a distant star in the firmament, and as we ascended higher, it became larger and larger, until its cheering rays shot down upon the ladder-steps, gladdening our hearts more than the sweetest music. Firmly grasping the last ladder, we felt the tears of thankfulness stealing into our eyes; and reaching the topmost round, and stepping into the dazzling light, we had to wipe them away with the sleeve of our flannel dress. But for the pick-handle I shudder at the result. We were saved by the guiding hand of our Heavenly Father out of the darksome dungeon into the blessed air and glorious sunshine! By untiring, persevering effort, we had climbed into the light.

During one of her public lectures at Launceston, the late Mrs. C. L. Balfour read several of my minor poems contained in the second edition of my "Lays from the Mine, the Moor, and the Mountain," the only volume then published, which were heartily received. The one headed, "The Mother's Teaching," was rendered so beautifully by her, that her hearers were greatly delighted. "She read your pieces so deliciously," said one in the audience, "that you would scarcely have known your own poems." She also spoke pleasantly of me and my little book, repeating the same in a letter to the late Rev. John Gostick, to whom I was in the habit of reciting my earlier effusions. She thus wrote to him July 29, 1856:—

"Many thanks for your kindness in sending me the volume of sweet poems by Mr. Harris. I will without delay write to Scotland, and endeavour to put in train some method of getting the work so reviewed as to help the worthy and gifted author. You did not tell me the price of the volume in case I am able to obtain any orders among my circle at home. Have you sent a copy to Messrs. Chambers? I rather think young Gerald Massey reviews poetry for Chambers' Journal. He did when I was in Edinburgh last spring. In the midst of the mysticism and imitation of Tennyson, that pervades so much of our modern poetry, it is refreshing to read the clear thoughts sweetly expressed from the 'Moor and the Mine.' A lady at Launceston after the lecture asked me the name of the Cornish Miner Poet, and for the moment I could not think of it."

This encouraged me as a timid beginner, and did me no small service. To take a poor toiling miner by the hand, while so many wondering ones stood aloof, was an act of Christian generosity which I feel I cannot praise too highly. After this she frequently corresponded with me, her letters being always full of loving sympathy and good cheer; and the first post-office-order I ever received came from her. She came to visit us at Falmouth, bringing her husband with her, and was interested to hear how I had sometimes in boyhood picked up a fragment of slate by the roadside, when a verse had suddenly visited me, and scratched it thereon with the point of an iron nail; nor was she less interested in the information that the bulk of my father's library consisted in the "Pilgrim's Progress," "Charles Wesley's Hymns," and the "Bible." When she died, I felt I had lost a true friend; and my elegy on her removal may be found in the British Workman for 1878.

"The Love of Home," which was the leading poem in my first book, and is the opening one in my "Wayside Pictures," was chiefly composed out of doors when coming and going to my mine-work. A great many of the word-pictures here are drawn from real life. The Aged Pilgrim was an old man who lived in a thatched cottage near my father, whose house fell down when I was a boy. The Old Soldier was my own uncle Bill, who used to tell me his adventures with an endless echo. The Cot among the Trees was our old home on the hill; and the Parting Scene was what I witnessed there. The Miller was suggested by a peasant's abode in the neighbourhood, where the meadow hedges were partly built, and the fields half-cultivated, he having suddenly emigrated to the gold region. The Bard's Daughter in the "War Fiend," is my own little maid now in heaven. The quiet dingle which we frequently visited in the twilight to see the glow-worms is still dear to my memory. It was interesting to meet with two young Cornishmen, one having written off my Walks with the Wild Flowers from a borrowed copy, and the other having learnt by heart my Love of Home.

I now began in my leisure to prepare pieces for a second volume. One evening Mr. Edward Bastin knocked at our door. He had often written me before, and had now heard of a Scripture Reader being required at Falmouth. Dear good man! He had walked three miles forth, and three miles back in the twilight to tell me of it. He acted as kindly as a father, and at last procured the situation for me, where I have been for the last twenty-four years. Had I remained in the mine I could not have survived until now, so that Mr. Bastin's efforts have prolonged my life. It was very gratifying about this time to visit Penjerrick, the lovely residence of the late R. W. Fox, Esq., F.R.S., and to take tea with his household from a silver teapot, the ore being raised in Dolcoath mine, from which I had been so recently released. Soon after coming to Falmouth, I published my "Land's End, Kynance Cove, and other Poems." This was in 1858. A copy of this little book of one hundred and eighty pages became the property of an unappreciative possessor. It was sold at a public auction with a surplus of household wares, and the purchaser posted it to a lady-friend of his in a distant part of the country. She was so pleased with some of the domestic pieces therein contained, that, as an acknowledgement of her delight and thorough appreciation, she forwarded me half-a-sovereign, thereby counteracting the mental apathy of a careless proprietor, and cheering me under a cloud of neglect. In 1860 came my "Mountain Prophet, the Mine, and other Poems." During the summer of this year, Edward Capern, the Devonshire Poet, spent a week with me. We visited several places of local interest, and passed the time most agreeably. He sang his own songs, composed his pieces, and praised our land of mines and moors. He thoroughly enjoyed the beauties of nature and the loveliness of truth; and I doubt if a truer poet ever existed.

My first visit to Kynance Cove was in the harvest of 1855, soon after the publication of my first book. A neighbour was kind enough to grant his conveyance, and some half-a-dozen of us went thither by the way of Nine Maidens and Helston. It was a breezy drive over wide moors and through honeysuckled lanes, where swallows floated and twittering birds made pleasant melody, more delicious to me as having escaped for a brief season from the sulphur and strain of the mine. It is impossible to describe the joyousness I felt in the full freedom of Nature, after being for several months in succession toiling day after day underground. Several miles south of Helston we came upon the strata of serpentine for which this locality is so famous, indications of which were plainly visible around us. Some of the house-fronts were built with this polished stone, and the road over which we drove was composed of the same material, and was exceedingly smooth, so that the carriage glided over it as if on ice. I was greatly struck with the beautiful heather growing on the hedges and marshes, and had to leave the vehicle several times to procure specimens. And when the polished crags of the Cove, with its white sands, and limpid pools, first burst upon my vision, the wonder of my soul was too great for words. It seemed like some fairy palace which the next sounding wave would sweep away. The music of the billows among the shining breakers, and the flight of the sea-birds from peak to peak glittering in the sun, revealed to me a region of enchantment like that which comes in dreams; and I returned to my home overjoyed with the fact that my own dear county produced such an exquisite picture. This day's revel among the scaly groups of serpentine, where the goddess of Beauty was reflected in the glassy deep, issued in my "Kynance Cove."

In 1863, I published "A Story of Carn Brea, Essays, and Poems." A short lyric in this book—The Dying Minstrel—called forth the following tender letter from the pen and heart of a now deceased lady. It was forwarded to my valued friend, the late Edmund Fry, and is herewith published for the first time:—

"Please kindly convey to Mr. Harris my warm acknowledgements for his exquisite verses. They are truly beautiful, and I prize them more than I can express. True-hearted sympathy is very sweet and comforting to those who suffer. But O! my friend, that heavenly city—golden city shining far away—what fulness of spiritual communion, what perfection of intelligence will be there! Kindred spirits will converse together as they never could on earth. John Harris will be there, and I shall know him and thank him as I cannot now. I am going out for awhile this bright afternoon. A new and peculiar charm invests this lovely world of ours as I gaze upon it thinking that in all probability it is the last time I shall see it in its spring and summer dress. All things have a solemn beauty that I never felt before. The melody of birds, the harp-like music of the winds, seem laden with mystic voices, songs like legends strange to hear! Adieu. MARIA J. E. FOTHERBY."

My brother, writing me from Michigan, North America, says that one of the essays in this volume was the means of the conversion to Christianity of a very careless man in that country—an event it is a pleasure to record.

In 1866, I published "Shakespere's Shrine, an Indian Story, Essays and Poems; and in 1868, "Luda, a Lay of the Druids, Hymns, Tales, Essays, and Legends." Up to this time Doctor Smith acted for me with my London printer, I collecting the money from my subscribers, and he forwarding it: and about this time he died. The Doctor's kindness was a relief to me, as I could take my own time about it. But to get subscribers, what a tug! what a battle with the Fates! what excuses! what refusals! what disdains! And a positive objection to patronize my pieces cut me like a thrice-sharpened sword. Often has my heart been more heavy than I can express, when the wealthy have turned their backs upon me, declining to take a single 2/6 copy of my works. O, anything, anything else but a poor poet and his books! "Nobody reads your poems," said one of our proud people to me; and without giving a cheerful order, stalked off to his dinner of roast. I confess at this time that I thought my last book was published. I saved every penny to pay my bills, denying myself continually; and up to this period I had scarcely profited a solitary pound, fed only with the faint breath of fame. The struggle to get subscribers was just as bitter as blasting the rock in the mine, it being generally looked upon as a charity. Large numbers of my pieces were written at this time when going to and returning from my visits to the poor of the Falmouth Union Workhouse.

The tide began to turn a little, however, with my Shakespere watch, though it took some time to make it known through my published works. The winning of the Tercentenary Prize happened thus. A rhyming friend of mine, Mr. W. Catcott, sent me an advertisement cut from a London journal, wherein was offered the prize of a gold watch for the best poem on the three hundredth anniversary of the birth of Shakespere, advising me to compete for it. I consulted my wife about it, and she thought it would be well to try. So try I did, writing and copying my ode in two evenings by the kitchen fire when the children were sleeping in bed. Up to this time I had no place of study or retirement. I complied with the requirements of the committee, sending my poem with a motto only, and my own name with a similar motto in a sealed envelope. Before posting it, however, I read it to my wife, and she spoke encouragingly of it. It would be nearly three months before the poems would be examined by the adjudicators, and so we had to wait. Time passed, and I had forgotten the day of competition, going out at my Bible reading. When I came in, my wife called to me from the top of the stairs, "You have won the prize—the gold watch." And sure enough there was a telegram asserting that I was the successful competitor out of upwards of one hundred. I was invited to Coventry, to participate in the presentation; but that could not be. For this entertainment great preparation had been made. Flags were hung in the streets, and the shopkeepers closed their shops at five in the evening. The Corn Exchange was pleasingly decorated. The back of the orchestra was ornamented with crimson drapery, the city arms and choice flowering shrubs. In the centre was a *fac-simile* of the bust of Shakespere over his grave in Stratford Church. Wreaths, garlands, and flags were arranged about the hall in tasteful profusion, and the pillars were ornamented by scrolls, inscribed with the names of Shakespere's works. The Mayor of the city, the Mayor's crier and macebearer wore their official costume, and his Worship announced from the platform that the first prize had been gained by my poor self.

In three or four weeks the postman brought it. He gave his usual knock at the door, and handed in the box, saying, "I verily believe the little fellow is come." He came into the kitchen, nor would he leave until he had seen the case opened, and its contents spread before his eyes. Then he danced around the room, clapped his hands and shouted, "We have beaten them all! Hurrah! hurrah! The *barbarians* of Cornwall are at the very top of the tree! Huzza! huzza!" The watch was greatly admired by all. On the centre of the case is engraven a beautiful representation of Shakespere, encircled with a wreath of leaves, and surrounded with the words, "The Tercentenary of Shakespere, 1864." Inside the case are engraven those well-known lines from the great bard:—

> "To-morrow, and to-morrow, and to-morrow
> Creeps in this petty pace, from day to day,
> To the last syllable of recorded time."

The newspapers published an account of it, letters of congratulation reached me from various quarters, and many who had scarcely spoken to me before saluted me most heartily. "This is John Harris, the Cornish Poet," said a lady to an official who was showing us the Abbey at Bath; but he scarcely lifted his eyes to my face. "This is John Harris," said she, "who won the Shakespere Prize;" and he took off his hat and bowed. My few friends and supporters were bound more closely to me; and I found myself, for a while at least, an object of no small distinction. In a public meeting in my own village of Troon, Doctor George Smith thus expressed himself. "There is a great ado about this gold watch, and it is all right. But there is one thing about it I do not like. In all the newspapers that

I have seen, he is called John Harris, of *Falmouth*. But he is not John Harris, of Falmouth—he is OUR John Harris, and we mean to keep him." The MS. poem, which the late Lord Lyttelton designated "remarkable," is now glazed and framed, by Mr. Vincent, and preserved in the Shakespere Museum, Stratford-on-Avon, which is supposed to be the only working man's literary contribution in the place. Mr. William Hooper and I visited Stratford in November, 1864, after I had won the gold watch, which was competed for by the United Kingdom and also by America.

Though I am now sixty-one years of age, I have never been out of Cornwall but once. This was in 1864, just after I had won the gold watch before alluded to, in company with W. Hooper, Esq. The whir of the train made me ill, from which I soon recovered, and was all the better for the change. We visited Bristol, Clifton, Hereford, Worcester, Gloucester, Malvern, Birmingham, and Stratford-upon-Avon. The latter place bound me with a wondrous spell. I seemed to be walking in some enchanted garden, where every tree and flower and sunny fountain gleamed with a splendour not of earth; and the music which rose from river and ravine was more than can be uttered. I stole into Shottery like one in a dream, and seemed to hear a volume of sweet voices which sounded centuries before. The very motion of the twigs was melody, and the click of the garden gate a song. This delightful journey issued in my producing eleven lyrics, viz., "Out of Cornwall," "Shakespere's Shrine," "Shakespere's House," "Shottery,"

"Shakespere's Tomb," "The Avon," "The Winding Wye," (this piece is set to music) "The Monument of Chatterton," "Visit to a Poet's Family," "Malvern in the Mist," and "George Muller." These pieces were first published in 1866, and most of them have been re-produced in my "Wayside Pictures." This first and last ramble out of my native county is a very pleasant reminiscence, and gave me exalted ideas of the vast wealth of England; though I stretched forth my hands to dear old Cornwall as the loveliest spot of earth.

In 1870, I published "Bulo, Reuben Ross, A Tale of the Manacles, Hymn, Song, and Story." This book was dedicated to Robert Alexander Gray, Esq., who behaved exceedingly kind, so that the edition was soon disposed of, and I became the possessor of a score or two of pounds. Through his influence I made the acquaintance of several good people in London, who were friendly ever afterwards. In 1872, I brought out "The Cruise of the Cutter, and other Peace Poems," which was dedicated to the Baroness Burdett Coutts, who had long subscribed to my writings, and to whom I owe very much. I submitted these MSS. to a publishing house in London, asking them if they would bring it out for me. They replied that poetry would not sell; but if I would undertake to dispose of 350 copies, they would publish the work. I agreed; and before it was out of the press had sold the whole edition. This was my first appeal to the publishers, and my last. At the suggestion of Mr. John Gill, of Penryn, I commenced, in 1873, a series of social illustrated tracts, under the heading of "Peace Pages for the People," advocating arbitration instead of war. Twenty-four of these four-paged papers were published by Mr. Gill, who distributed many thousands of them gratuitously in various Sunday schools throughout the country. Several of these tracts have been reprinted in America. I have also written upwards of thirty religious tractates for different houses, besides a large number of essays and articles for various periodicals. In 1874, I collected some of my best pieces into a large crown quarto volume, double-columned, with a portrait, and published it under the title of "Wayside Pictures, Hymns, and Poems." To do this I had to make many sacrifices which will never be chronicled. This volume I also dedicated to Mr. Gray, without whose generous help I could not have issued it. The expenses of printing this large book were upwards of £160, and my subscribers got the volume of me at 10/6. But several friends paid me a guinea a copy, and Mr. Gray himself sold more than £50 worth, so that I was not out of pocket by it. Dear Mr. Gray! Even while I write this they are laying him to rest in Forest Hill Cemetery, and the muffled bells of St. Giles's are pealing his funeral dirge. After a life of rare Christian goodness he fell asleep in peace in his ninetieth year. He was instrumental in procuring grants for me, in 1872-5, from the Royal Literary Fund, of £50. Chiefly with this sum I built a little study for myself over our kitchen; and in October, 1874, when I was 53 years of age, realized what I had been anxiously desiring for a lifetime.

Throughout the years 1875-6, Mr. J. E. M. Vincent employed me to write for him. He was the editor of two weeklies printed and published in Leamington. I worked diligently in the evenings, and in my hours of leisure, and produced a large number of articles, chiefly on the land question; several of which ran through the both papers, and I have reason to believe they were well received. The most ambitious of my performances was a serial in sixty-three chapters, entitled "Mountain Mat and his Three Sons," which was concluded on the 14th of November, 1876. Its title, however, was changed before the story was completed, to suit the purpose of the editor. It dealt largely with the reclamation of waste lands, and embraced many of the incidents of my boyhood and youth. It still remains unpublished, save in the newspaper form, and looks as if it were likely to be lost for ever.

My next work was "Walks with the Wild Flowers," published in 1875, and dedicated to Earl Northbrook, then Governor-General of India. His friendship has been of great value to me, which still continues. The edition was soon sold. In 1877, I brought out my "Tales and Poems," a miscellaneous work of 186 pages 8vo. I had prepared another volume for the printer, even to the writing of the preface, when on Sunday evening, April 14, 1878, without any premonitory symptoms, I was suddenly laid low with a stroke of paralysis. For two months I was confined to the house, but on June 17 re-commenced my Scripture-reading labours. My salary was, however, in the midst of my prostration, very much reduced. Through this great lessening of my income I have borne much privation, not the least part being, for a season, the loss of my little study. This can only be rightly understood by those who for so long a period have been sighing after solitude. To possess for three years what I so ardently desired from boyhood almost to old age, and then to lose it suddenly in the midst of sickness, was no easy cross to bear, though now it is given up entirely for the sake of my invalid son. At the end of this year I brought out my "Two Giants," wherein I attacked the monster evils of drink and war. This volume contains my autobiography, to which I have added considerably in the present issue. The little book of 130 pages was very kindly received, and the edition was soon exhausted. It contained some dedicatory stanzas to Earl Northbrook, to whom the volume is respectfully inscribed.

In 1879, I published "Monro," crown 8vo., pages 152. This volume contains a reprint of the Shakespere Ode, which won the Tercentenary watch in 1864, and which I have now usefully worn for the last eighteen years. The late Professor Longfellow thus wrote me on receipt of the volume:—

"Cambridge, January 13, 1880. My dear Sir. I have had the pleasure of receiving your friendly letter, and the volume of poems you have had the kindness to send me. I hasten to thank you for both. I shall read this volume with deep interest and sympathy; for I see by the preface and by the arguments of the several books, that it is your life. The thought uppermost in my mind at this moment is, what a divine benediction the gift of song must have been to you through all your laborious life. How dark your way would have been without it! How luminous it has been with it! Thank God for the gift of song. I rejoice to see the cordiality of the newspaper notices you sent me. Your poems are hailed with universal applause. One does not care for indiscriminate praise, but one does care for considerate recognition. With all good wishes for the New Year, I am, my dear Sir, faithfully yours, Henry W. Longfellow."

I scarcely need say how true the Professor's words are. Without the pursuit of poetry my life would have been weariness indeed, but with it trials and severe hardships have been transformed into blessings. The Professor again wrote me respecting my "Wayside Pictures."

"My dear Sir. I have had the pleasure of receiving your letter, and the copy of 'Wayside Pictures,' for both of which please accept my sincere and cordial thanks. This volume, which embodies so much of your life, I shall read from time to time, as I have leisure; for without leisure, and faculties disengaged from other work, no one can properly read poetry. Meanwhile, I will endeavour to have notices of the volume taken by the papers. If I were a critic, and writer of reviews, I would do it myself. But that is a field I never enter. Wishing you, in the words of your English Selden, 'contenting enjoyments of your auspicious desires, and a happy attendance of your chosen Muses,' I am, my dear Sir, yours very truly, Henry W. Longfellow."

In October, 1881, I published "Linto and Laneer," crown 8vo., pages 174. Of this book Mr. S. C. Hall, F.S.A., writes me thus:—

"My dear Sir. I have read many of the poems contained in your book entitled 'Linto and Laneer'—read them with very great pleasure. They are thoroughly well-written, graceful and often beautiful as compositions. As mere poems I rank them very high But that is their least—at all events not their principal—merit. They inculcate the higher duties of humanity—love of God, and love of man, advocating the loftiest and holiest love of both, teaching much that cannot be learned without vast profit to heart, mind, and soul. Yet they can hardly be called didactic; certainly if they are sermons, it is in the sense that sermons may be found in stones, and good in everything. The subjects are so varied, the treatment so touching, the moral so simply natural, that I feel gratified in accepting this little volume as one of the most remarkable of its class and order I have ever read. I believe that to aid its circulation would be not only to give pleasure, but to advance and strengthen the cause of morality, religion, and all the social virtues. With the best wishes for your health, happiness, and prosperity; and thanking you for another pleasure added to the pleasures I have so often received from pure, simple, graceful, and instructive verse, I am truly and faithfully yours, S. C. Hall, November 11, 1881."

While this little book has been passing through press, Mr. Hall has written me as follows:—

"You are a good and industrious man, as well as a man of much ability; and the world ought to have used you better than it has done."

From December, 1879, to the end of August, 1880, I had written nearly one hundred original poems. My "Walks with the Wild Flowers," "Tales and Poems," "The Two Giants," and "Monro," have been illustrated by my son Alfred. All my books have been published by subscription, and on my own responsibility, so that my whole life has been one of earnest labour. I lost several pounds through one of my city publishers becoming bankrupt; and from the year 1860 to the present time have only received £3. 1s. 1d. through my London booksellers. The friendship of Mr. Clapp (Tenax Exon) has been pleasant to me. The expenses from first to last in connection with my book-publishing cannot be less than a thousand pounds, and I should have but little in the shape of money to encourage me, were it not for a grant from the Royal Bounty Fund, through the late Earl Beaconsfield, in April,

1877, of £200. This was greatly owing to the untiring efforts of W. H. Northy, Esq., kindly assisted by John Tremayne, Esq., M.P., the Right Hon. the Earl of Mount Edgcumbe, and the Right Hon. John Bright. I unfortunately lodged the entire grant in the Cornish Bank here, and on its suspension some two years afterwards lost a serious portion of it. In September, 1881, the Right Hon. W. E. Gladstone, through the representation of Earl Northbrook, aided by T. Webber, Esq., made me a second grant from the Civil List of £100. In the beginning of 1879, I was elected a Fellow of the Royal Historical Society. Dr. Rogers, writing me respecting my "Monro," says:—

"You are a true poet. I read your book with the greatest pleasure and interest. Unlike many Scottish poets who consider tippling a concomitant of genius, you have conducted yourself well, and gained public favour both as a man and as an author. I hold you in much respect, and sincerely hope that every blessing, temporal and spiritual, may attend you. Yours most faithfully, Charles Rogers."

An old account-book of my father's has recently been put into my hands, in which is the following entry of mine, made in the home of my parents when I was a little more than twenty-one years of age:—August 2, 1842. I this day resolve to devote Mondays and Wednesdays to grammar, Tuesdays to history, or such books as I may have from the (Sunday school) library, Thursdays to poetry-reading, Fridays composition, Saturdays miscellaneous works, and Sundays theology. Thus I intend, by the help of the Master, to improve the golden moments as they pass. O may He enlighten me by His Holy Spirit, and guide me by His counsel, that my days may not be spent in vain! While I strive to obtain worldly knowledge, may I endeavour to become acquainted with the things belonging to my peace, and may my literary acquirements be devoted to the honour and glory of God.

Since my first boyish bursts in my father's barn, I have written upwards of a thousand pieces of prose and rhyme. And though my life has been one of hardship and severe struggle, I have been content. A crust and a song is better than a sirloin and a groan. I have given the world my thoughts of fifty years, and I am thankful. And although I have written upwards of a hundred Gospel hymns, offering them to any section of the Christian Church, and not one, that I know of, has yet found its place in any collection, I will not despair of their being appreciated one day, and becoming humble vessels fit for the Master's use. The Rev. S. W. Christophers, in his "Poets of Methodism," relates the following pleasing incident respecting one of my hymns. A miner had been worshipping God in a little chapel at the foot of the hill, and was requested by a visitor on the way to his cottage to tell him the secret of his success:—

"I suppose," said he, "it is because we are thrifty, content with wholesome food, and decent clothes. I believe the great secret is that we have learnt to love God, and to let Him manage for us. A few years ago, some of our men were tempted to go to South America, for the sake of getting a little fortune. They wanted me to go with them; but I began to think whether it was right to risk my life, to leave my wife, and, above all, to risk my soul to go to a country full of temptation, and with no helps to piety, all for gold. I prayed about it, and reasoned the matter before God. And I believe I was helped to make up my mind by a blessed little hymn that was made by John Harris, who used to work at Dolcoath, a miner like myself, and knowing by experience the trials of a miner. The hymn was 'The Lord shall choose for me.' I used to go about humming to myself, now one verse and then another, till at last I made up my mind to abide in the house of the Lord at home, and trust Him who had always so far provided for me and mine. My comrades went. They made their fortunes, as the people say, but they lost their souls. Everything failed with me; and I was tempted to reflect upon myself for stopping home. But the Lord knew my motive, and I cried to Him in my distress. I had a rising family, and nothing for them. I cried for help, and soon got enough in a month to put me into comfortable circumstance. Not that I was rich, except in Christ. But I have brought up my nine children, given them decent schooling, and taught them to get an honest living. To this day, I have never wanted bread on my table, a fire on my hearth, or the blessing of a happy, contented home. Thank God!"

Mr. Christophers thus writes of my now sainted mother:—

"A passing visit to the poet's widowed mother, who was calmly waiting for her summons to Paradise, in a village not far from her son's birth-place, can never be forgotten. The old woman, more than three score years and ten, still retained in her person enough to show that her son John had inherited from her his most marked and expressive features. She was evidently a woman used to deep communings with herself and the spiritual world, and rejoiced in hope of her heavenly rest."

After a very brief illness she died in great peace, at Troon, Camborne, on Saturday morning, September 17th, 1881, at the ripe age of 82. To her daughter Kitty, who was with her in her last moments, she expressed herself as having no fear —none at all. She anticipated great joy in meeting her long-lost friends in heaven, and in seeing Jesus her Redeemer and Saviour. For more than

DEATH OF MY MOTHER.

fifty years she was a consistent member of a religious community, serving God in humbleness and fear without any pretence or show. She was buried at Treslothan, near Pendarves, where our youngest daughter has been sleeping under the green grass for the last twenty-seven years. A few humble neighbours bore her to her resting-place among the solemn pines, when the autumn leaves were falling, and the hush of twilight fell upon the earth; and at sixty-one years of age I lost the gentlest mother the world ever saw.

> Sleep on dear mother! death can do no more:
>   From earthly ills set free,
> Thou art a watcher on the quiet shore
>   Where God's own angels be.
>
> They bore thee to the traveller's house of rest
>   When Autumn filled the wheat,
> And the first dry leaves from his fading vest
>   Rustled beneath our feet.
>
> In nature's silence thou thy rest did'st take,
>   And then was heard the prayer,
> Like holy seraphs harping o'er the lake,
>   Upon the evening air.
>
> And days of old came back, with skies of blue,
>   And seas like crystal clear,
> When first I sang, where dearest wildings grew,
>   To please thy listening ear.
>
> Above thee rock the pines when winds are out,
>   And robin wakes his strain,
> And meek-eyed flowers are scattering scents about,
>   Like those adown the lane.
>
> The birds will twitter here the whole day long,
>   And larks above thee sing,
> And happy children list the wood's wild song
>   When buds come out in spring.

> How different here, where sounds the rustic reed,
>   When shepherds seek the fold,
> And sharp scythes rustle in the grassy mead,
>   Than in the city cold!
>
> So sleep thee, mother, while I travel on
>   Through tears that will not stay:
> Thy hand no more, as in dear seasons gone,
>   Can wipe those drops away!
>
> But oft, when Eve puts on her dusky veil.
>   And twilight fills the sky,
> Amid the mystery of the silent dale
>   Thy wings shall murmur by.

From the publication of my first volume until now my principal aim has been to elevate mankind; and this shall bias my future meditations, with the help of the Divine Giver, until "the silver cord is loosed, and the golden bowl is broken."

I have often been cheered in my life-struggle with the remembrance of that beautiful allegorical poem of the late Professor Longfellow, wherein he describes a young man wandering among the mountains of the Alps, bearing in his hand a banner, upon which is written this strange device, "Excelsior." This young man is represented by the poet as beginning to climb one of those mighty mountains, on whose crest is eternal winter, bearing this strange banner in his hand; when he is met by a peasant, who endeavours to dissuade him from the task. But glancing at the banner, "Higher, and yet higher still," he leaves the peasant behind him, and hastens on his way. Farther up, on the rough ridges of the kingly mount, he meets with another traveller, who tries to discourage him, and persuade him to go back. But once more he gazes at the banner, "Higher and yet higher still," and with eager footsteps he climbs towards the stars, from white snow-field to snow-field, higher and higher from this wicked world, till a wanderer, toiling through the snow, finds him lying in the winds, with the mark of death upon his forehead, still grasping the banner in his icy hand; and over him, high up in the blue fields of ether, a spirit is singing sweetly—tis the spirit of the youth still chanting the word, "Excelsior." To the young especially let me say, Emblazon the word "Excelsior" on your banner, "higher and yet higher still." Go forth with it into the world, act under its dictates, and circumstances shall bend before you. Aim at a certain object, turn your steps towards it perseveringly, hopefully, cheerfully; and by and by you shall be crowned with the laurel. Christian! emblazon the word "Excelsior" on thy banner, "higher, and yet higher still." Heed not those who would entice thee to go back; keep thine eye on the crown before thee; walk in the footprints of thy blessed Redeemer; rear aloft thy standard, "Higher, and yet higher still," and soon the ivory palaces of heaven will be thy home. Let us take this motto as our burning, living watchword, "Higher, and yet higher still:" higher in Christian experience, higher in the knowledge of God, higher in the Divine life, higher in the scale of existence, higher in acts of benevolence, and deeds of good-will towards our fellow-creatures, "higher, and yet higher still," till we climb the green hills of Eden, and gather flowers in the fields of light.

GLOSSARY.

COBBING HOUSE...*Where the mineral is cobbed, or beaten, from the dead stones.*

FLOORS ....*The space assigned to the dressed ores, when prepared for the market.*

HUTCH.................*Where the fine ores are sifted in water, and prepared for the market.*

KEEVE.................*A hooped barrel, half-filled with water, where the rough mineral is washed in a sieve.*

MAN-ENGINE ......*A machine to let the workmen up and down the mine.*

PICKING TABLE...*Where the valuable ores are picked out, and the refuse thrown away.*

PLOT ....*An excavation in the side of the shaft, having a floor of wood, where the broken earth is shovelled into the bucket.*

SINK ....*A kind of well.*

SLIDE ....*The compartment where the mineral is trammed when drawn to the surface.*

TIN-STOPE............*A stair-cut excavation over or under a level.*

TRIBUTER ....*One who labours for a certain portion of the mineral he may discover.*

UNPUBLISHED POEMS.

THE DAISY MEADOW.

DEAR image of the dainty Spring!
  My heart is cheered by thee;
One scene which thou wert sure to bring
  Is evermore with me,—
A meadow of my father's farm,
  Where I would roam for hours,
With my dear harp upon my arm,
  All white with daisy flowers.

Twas called by us the Under Field,
  And there the lambkins played,
When violet-fairies donned their shield
  In many a mossy glade.
But nought to me was half so dear,
  Which loving Nature dowers,
As this small meadow by the mere
  All white with daisy flowers.

The hum of insects met my ear,
  The gorse in gold was dressed,
And underneath the hawthorn near
  The robin built its nest;
The lark his sweetest song did yield,
  Which fell in liquid showers:
O, nought was like the Under Field
  All white with daisy flowers.

In ranks behind, in ranks before,
   They wooed the summer air,
A countless host. a starry floor,
   They kissed each other there.
And even now my heart is healed,
   Though sorrows come in showers,
When thinking of the Under Field
   All white with daisy flowers.

It comes in evening's twilight dreams,
   When song is on the floods,
And music in unnumbered streams
   Floats through the leafy woods.
With charms to deaden worldly care,
   And melt the cloud which lowers,
The Under Field, where hides the hare,
   All white with daisy flowers.

Nor will it fade from memory's eye,
   From memory's treasured store,
Till darkness shadow earth and sky,
   And life itself is o'er.
A bliss by hidden hands unsealed,
   To cheer my latest hours,
Is that hill-sloping Under Field
   All white with daisy flowers.

MY EARLY HOME.

WHEN starting tears are in mine eye,
And rises oft the bursting sigh,
When careless words oppress my soul,
And noisy tongues of torture roll,
My thoughts, unfettered, fly at will
To my dear cottage on the hill.

When I am weary with life's march,
Beneath some pride-erected arch,
Where pipers play, whose numbers roar
Like potsherds grating on the shore,
The lark is with me sweetly-shrill
Above the heather of my hill.

When I am wandering sadly on,
My lyre unstrung, its music gone,
Where sounds of anguish fill my ears,
And sorrow's face is stained with tears,
The rustling ferns, the rippling rill,
Are with me on my dear old hill.

And when, like Jonah, low I lie,
And feel t'were better far to die,
My earth-gourds gone, my props decayed,
And dry wells open in the glade,
A solace for my sorrows still
Is my dear boulder-covered hill.

When ranked with those who scarcely know
Why oceans ebb, or currents flow,
To whom the printer's page is less
Than flounces on my lady's dress,
With gushing drops my eyes will fill
For years of music on the hill.

And ask you why I ever turn
To these lone heights so still and stern?
A mother there, a father good,
And brothers mid the thyme-banks stood,
Where Nature gave her child his quill,
And God is on my native hill.

THE BRIGHT PATH.

ONE track is like a track of gold,
    My boyhood's feet have trod,
Tis with me up and down the earth,
    Wherever I may plod,
In budding spring, in summer time,
    And when the winds are cool,—
The narrow path through Rickard's Moor,
    That led to Forest school.

The moss-cups on the violet banks,
   The brooklet glancing clear,
Were whispering like the voice of Love
   When primrose-tufts appear.
O, I was taught by birds that fly,
   And fishes in the pool
Beside the path through Rickard's Moor
   That led to Forest school.

Down hill we ran with nimble feet
   Among the furze and heath,
Where, mid the masses of bog-peat,
   The rushes shone beneath.
I left my mother at her task,
   My marbles by the stool,
To tread the path through Rickard's Moor
   That led to Forest school.

And now I seem to hear again
   The tinkle of the stream,
The lark's song o'er the sunny bowers
   Where fern-hid fairies dream;
To tread once more the springy turf,
   Where brooklets murmur cool,
Along the path through Rickard's Moor
   That led to Forest school.

What is it in the human heart
   That chance and change outlives,
Unconquered by the crush of years?
   The love which Nature gives.
Yet more and more this narrow track
   Gleams by the rushy pool
Along the path through Rickard's Moor
   That led to Forest school.

TEMPTATION RESISTED.

A CRUSH of crags, distorted as with pain,
   Piled on the barren moor,
Where winds wail ever in the hissing rain
   From midnight's shadowy shore.

One star burnt half-way up the black concave,
   There was no other gleam,
Twas ghostly—ghastly as a ruined nave
   Where owls in concert scream.

When lo! an object left a horrid rent,
   Where moonlight never steals;
His cloak was blacker than the night's descent,
   Which reached his hideous heels.

One smutty hand he lifted as he came;
   The boulders seemed to nod,
When he exclaimed, "I give thee wealth and fame,
   If thou wilt leave thy God."

"No, wretch," I cried. "The King shall have my all,
   The warblings of my lyre,
Though on life's highway with my crutch I fall,
   Or sink in flood and fire.

"I'll sing His praises who endured the cross,
   Who lived, who died for me,
Though with the world I suffer pain and loss,
   And crumbs my portion be."

The black arm fell, the ebon robe grew less,
   The monster dwindled fast,
And with this echo, "Heaven is sweet redress,"
   Into the night he passed.

THE PRAYING MOTHER.

A PLEASING sight, which angels love,
   And God delights to see,
In this cold world of sin and self,
   Where numerous evils be,
And multitudes, with fruitless aim,
   Make filmy husks their fare,
Leaving the living Bread of Life
   For emptiness and air.

It haunts me now, when sitting here
    Beside my little fire,
Sweeping, with feeble hand and slow,
    My oft-awakened lyre.
The solemn woods are still to-night,
    The birds are gone to rest,
And every little lambkin lies
    Safe on its mother's breast.

The stars are out o'er primrose buds
    That slumber in the dell,
And mystic voices murmur by
    The moss-encircled well.
Yet that which I have seen to-day
    Will foremost with me stand,—
A mother kneeling low in prayer
    Among her household band.

Will not those scions of the hearth,
    Reared in affection's ray,
Grow up to benefit mankind,
    And walk in Wisdom's way?
O! England has ten thousand such
    Along our own dear land
Who love to kneel in earnest prayer
    Among their household band.

May they be greatly multiplied,
    From waning year to year,
Till every mother everywhere
    Act like this mother dear.
Her image oft shall cheer my soul
    Along life's silent sand,
When kneeling there in fervent prayer
    Among her household band.

THE REQUEST.

I HEAR far off diviner songs
    Than ever filled my soul
When boyhood roved, with careless feet,
    Where clearest waters roll.

THE REQUEST.

The echoes float with silver tongues
  O'er dearest lake and lea:
So, Cornwall, I have in my heart
  One thing to ask of thee.

I'm aged now, and stepping fast
  Towards the silent tomb,
Where all device is at an end,
  Nor flowers of fancy bloom.
My years have all been spent with thee,
  To song and silence wed,
And so I ask that thou would'st place
  Some wild flowers o'er my head.

Tis not a great thing, is it now,
  That I would humbly crave?
A few of Cornwall's hedgerow gems
  Upon my village grave!
The wild rose from the crooked lane,
  Beside the mossy well,
The cowslip and the violet,
  The primrose from the dell.

I've loved them long, I've loved them much,
  And now I love them more,
And surely I shall love them still
  When life and toil are o'er.
So through the mist of gathering tears,
  By holiest feeling led,
I ask that thou would'st nurture there
  The wild flowers o'er my head.

And when the dusk is on the hills,
  And in the listening vales,
And the bat round the belfry-eaves
  In airy circles sails,
I'll stoop from emerald heights unknown,
  Where love for ever sings,
And fan upon my silent grave
  The wild flowers with my wings.

THEOBRIGHT.

"The hay is cut, the swallows come,
  The summer flowers appear,
The lark is singing in the sky,
  And yet he is not here!
He should have come six months ago,
  'Twas thus the letter said:
Will Theobright be here again,
  Or is the sailor dead?"

"It is not, in this isle of change,—
  For all must feel it such,—
While travelling up and down the earth,
  Well to expect too much.
O, Susan, it is hard to say,
  And very sad when said,
But I believe, from what I hear,
  That Theobright is dead.

"His ship was viewed off Goldy's Point,
  When northern winds did roar,
Again they looked, but could not see
  His home-bound barque no more.
Some wreckage lined the Cornish coast;
  O, Susan, trust in God,
He knows what's best for every one,
  And rest upon His rod."

She bent her head, and seemed like one
  Who felt it good to pray;
And tears were gushing from her eyes,
  Which Willie wiped away.
"Don't cry, dear mother," sobbed the lad,
  "I've saved my ball and drum,
And Theobright shall have them both,
  When Theobright is come."

Next day the echoing Easter bells
  Were pealing on the air,
The cloth was laid, the table spread,
  The old man in his chair:

A footstep made them all look up,
  A tap was on the door,
And then a well-dressed youth came in
  And walked along the floor.

The old dame wiped her eyes again,
  And stood up by his side,
And Willie rushed into his arms,
  "'Tis Theobright!" he cried.
And Robin, mid the untouched meal,
  Knelt in his gladdened home,
And thanked the Lord with cheerful voice
  That Theobright was come.

DO THE BEST YOU CAN.

COURAGE, weary workers!
  'Tis not always dark,
Comes the welcome morning,
  Sings the soaring lark.
Eat your food with gladness,
  Aiding Nature's plan;
Give the world a whistle,
  Do the best you can.

Is it uphill with you
  Through a barren clime
Where no song is ringing?
  One step at a time.
Step by step will bring you
  To the summit, man,
Therefore hope—and onward,
  Do the best you can.

Do you share your morsels
  With dear Nell and Fred?
Are not their warm kisses
  Sweeter far than bread?

Nell will help you one day,
  Fred will be a man;
Give the world a whistle,
  Do the best you can.

Plough the straightest furrow,
  Pull the strongest oar,
Never mind the hardship
  When you reach the shore.
Ever in your efforts
  Aiding Nature's plan;
Give the world a whistle,
  Do the best you can.

LISTEN.

LISTEN, old man, listen!
  There is music still;
Hear it in the valley,
  Hear it on the hill.
Though thy youth is over,
  Still is heard the strain,
Which the mountains murmur,
  "Jesus Christ shall reign."

Listen, old man, listen!
  Love hath still a voice:
How the valleys echo!
  How the hills rejoice!
God's decree is certain,
  Come there joy or pain,
Earth shall be converted,
  Jesus Christ shall reign.

Listen, old man, listen!
  Every flower and tree,
Rill and rushing river,
  Has a voice for thee.
And when moonlight-tissues
  Span the village lane,
Sound the joyous tidings,
  "Jesus Christ shall reign."

Listen, old man, listen!
   War shall be no more,
The dread battle-giant
   Shall be drunk with gore.
Peace shall fill the highland,
   Peace shall fill the plain,
Earth be changed to Eden,
   Jesus Christ shall reign.

Listen, old man, listen!
   Scout the sceptic's creed,
Let the scoffer tremble,
   God's own Son did bleed.
Hell shall roar with anguish,
   Satan clank his chain,
Sin and death be conquered,
   Jesus Christ shall reign.

LIFE'S EVENING.

THE twilight gathers o'er the moss,
   Let's on till I the threshold cross,
Though worn and weary with my loss.

How fast the shadows hide the plain!
And from the heights I hear a strain,
Like that which comes with summer rain.

My staff is bent, my sandals worn,
My dusty garments stained and torn;
O, when will come that other morn!

The autumn winds have stript the tree,
And left the branches bare to see,
And weariness has hold of me.

The whispering children slowly say,
"That white old man has had his day,
And soon he will be called away."

The dells grow darker where I stand,
But He is here to hold my hand,
And guide me to the higher land.

The last lone vale will soon be trod,
My feet regain that other sod,
And I shall hear the bells of God.

HYMN.

JESUS, let me worship Thee
  Where the rocks and ruins be,
Where the sea its story tells
To the shining sands and shells,
Where the flowers in Nature's dome
Whisper of that higher home.

There Thy loving Spirit dwells
With the trees and flowerets' bells,
And the meditative mind,
Seeking Thee, shall surely find
Grace to help his varied lot
Where the foot of man is not.

By the fountain let me pray,
When the sunlight gilds the spray,
When the waters murmur low,
And Thy voice is in their flow,
Telling me of heaven restored
For the sake of Christ my Lord.

When the morning wakes the bird,
When the song of noon is heard,
When the evening dims the light,
When the stars come forth at night,
Under bush, by bower and tree,
Jesus, let me worship Thee.

A BIRTHDAY HYMN.

(Respectfully inscribed to Frederick Clapp, " Tenax Exon.")

LIKE a traveller on the road,
  Leading to his dear abode,
Left in childhood in the dell,
Near the moss-encircled well,
Gazing onward through his tears,
So thou view'st thy fifty years.

O'er thy path strange airs have swayed
Like the mystery of the glade.
O, what love thy Lord has shown,
As the months have onward flown,
Better than thy doubts and fears
During all thy fifty years!

He who guides us to the goal,
Asks the service of the soul,
Cheers us with His Spirit's light,
Claims our influence for the right.
How the Father's love appears,
Sparing thee those fifty years!

Not a trial has been sent,
Not a generous blessing lent,
Not a cross, or landscape bright,
But has been ordained aright,
By the Hand that rules the spheres,
Sparing thee those fifty years.

Pray, accept this verse from me,
On thy solemn Jubilee.
Keep thy hand to Friendship's oar,
Labour still to lift the poor,
Till the Son of Man appears,
Who has spared thee fifty years.

January 17th, 1870.

TESTIMONIAL VERSES.

To F. Clapp, (Tenax Exon) on the Presentation of a Gold Watch by his Exeter friends, January 17th, 1879.

THE man who lessens human woe,
    The tears which from affliction flow,
Who turns aside oppression's thrust,
And lifts the lowly from the dust,
Employing strength, and health, and store,
To bring new blessings to the poor,
Approaches nearer to his God
Than he who sways a kingly rod.

And such is he whose worth is known
In many a cot of roughest stone,
On floors were merry children play
In isles romantic far away,
Where sits the labourer at his board
To health and home and friends restored,
Whom we desire to honour now,
And place the green wreath on his brow.

In cities vast, and lowlands dim,
If selfish souls were more like him,
What flowers would spring where thistles grow,
And through the desert rivers flow,
Sweet songs arise from shire and shed,
Where Misery lies with restless head,
And plenty cheer each mother's child,
And beauty blossom on the wild!

And so upon life's homeward way
We crown him with our loves to-day,
As one who scatters light around
Wherever human hives are found,
Beseeching men to prize God's gift,
And practice industry and thrift.
As "Tenax Exon" in the gap,
We hail, we honour, FREDERICK CLAPP.

CONRAD AND THE STORK.

PART FIRST.

Conrad and his widowed mother
   Dwelt beneath a pine,
Where the gathered snows of Norway
   On the mountains shine.

And a stork came there each summer,
   From far lands immense,
Laid its eggs, and reared its young ones
   By the garden fence.

And they won the bird with kindness,
   Words and glances bland,
Till it came at Conrad's whistle,
   Feeding from his hand.

Every year the stork came winging,
   Just as Spring began,
Until Conrad in their cottage
   Grew into a man.

Then the ocean's restless billows
   Murmured in his sleep,
Till the youth became a sailor
   On the tossing deep.

All went well till pirates took them
   On the swelling waves,
Stript them, bound their limbs with fetters,
   Sold them all as slaves.

How his mother waited for him
   By the fireside lone,
Till her changing hair grew whiter,
   And all hope had flown!

How she prayed when night's dark mantle
    Fell on wood and wild,
And she heard her Saviour whisper,
    "I am with thy child!"

Still the stork came there each season,
    Causing her such joy;
So she watched it, wooed it, fed it,
    For her absent boy.

PART SECOND.

Conrad at his labour dreary
    Toiled till day was done,
When one noon a stork came wheeling
    Round him in the sun.

In a moment home and mother
    Rose before his eye;
Came the great stork at his whistle,
    As in days gone by.

Yes, it was the bird of boyhood,
    Which he then did see,
His dear stork which built in summer
    By their garden tree.

Conrad thanked the Lord for sending
    His true friend again:
So he wrote a loving letter,
    Very brief and plain;

Telling how the slave-man worked him
    Neath the sun's fierce ray;
To his dear stork's leg he tied it,
    Then it flew away.

To her lonely home in Norway,
   When the flowers expand,
Came the stork to cheer the widow,
   Feeding from her hand.

From its leg she took the letter;
   And who knows her joy
When she found the words were written
   By her long-lost boy!

Quickly spread the welcome tidings,
   Fast as news can run,
And the villagers united
   To redeem her son.

Money was subscribed in churches,
   Money came from all,
That poor Conrad might be purchased
   From the slave-man's thrall.

Soon a ship was sent to fetch him,
   Where the sunbeams burn;
And the bells were shortly ringing
   For his safe return.

In his humble Norway cottage
   Conrad sat once more:
His kind neighbours had redeemed him
   From the tyrant's shore.

How his mother loved to hear him,
   As he told his tale!
And their prayers and praises mingle
   When the dews prevail.

Earnest pleading is accepted,
   And shall pardon win;
Jesus has redeemed His people
   From the curse of sin.

THE MILLER AND HIS NAG.

WHAT a snug little place was the miller's abode,
    In a sycamore dell by the side of the road!
And his bright little boy from his cottage would steal,
And clap his small hands at the sound of the wheel.

The miller would hug him and kiss him once more,
Then point him to pony so sleek at the door,
Who never had lash-cord or leather-thong yet,
Since granny had called him the miller boy's pet.

He came at their call, he would feed from their hand,
And by the low stepping-block quietly stand,
Or carefully clamber the moorland ascent,
As the miller rode town-wards to settle his rent.

"I never beat pony," the miller would say,
"No matter how lengthened, how rugged the way;
A chirp or a whistle sufficeth for him,
Who trots on all day till the twilight is dim.

"A pat on his neck has more power than the lash,
And a kind word is stronger than oak-bough or ash.
So sing with the miller, who strikes not a blow,
'No whip for my pony wherever we go!'"

THE END.

From the RICHMOND *and* RIPON CHRONICLE, *January 28th, 1882.*

LIVING POETICAL WRITERS.

JOHN HARRIS.

John Harris is a poet of Nature's own making, and a genuine Cornishman. He now occupies the post of Scripture Reader at Falmouth; but from boyhood until long after he crossed the threshold of manhood he belonged to that class who have to beg a brother of the earth for leave to delve and toil. For many years his hands were brown with honest labour. By perseverance and industry he has gradually lifted himself up, and found a popular place in the annals of provincial literature. He is one remarkable instance of energy and ability triumphing over circumstances adverse to the cultivation of poetic talents. Moreover, he is a living signpost to others along the way to success, and absolute proof—if proof were wanting—that genius is as much the gift of the poor man as it is of the rich man, and that it buds and blossoms as well in a humble cottage as it does in a luxurious studio, or a castellated mansion.

John Harris was born on the 14th of October, 1820, so that he is more than sixty-one years of age. The place of his nativity was the top of Bolennowe Hill, Camborne, Cornwall. His father was a copper-miner and tributor. What education he got was at a school kept by one Dame Tregonza, and then an old man who used to punish the boys with a flat piece of hard wood studded thickly with sharp nails; and subsequently he attended a school taught by a miner named Roberts. At twelve years of age he went down into the mine with his father; and from that time until he became Scripture reader, his life was one of toil and intermittent struggle, enlivened only by the sweet breath of poetry. In his "Monro" he describes himself about this period of his life. He has already published fifteen volumes. "Monro" is a book of 148 pages. It takes its title from the principal poem in the book, which, in plain terms, is the poet's autobiography in verse. It is written in the Spenserian stanza, the same metre in which Byron has enshrined his "Don Juan." It is divided into three books; and throughout all the books the interest and charm of the narrative is well sustained. There are stanzas in the poem which so aptly describe nature pure and simple, that they stand out like Turner's. But a desultory quotation cannot give the reader an idea of the merit and charm of the poem. Every page has its smoothed rhythm and the breath of woodland flowers. The rest of the book is made up of miscellaneous poems, some of them of great merit.

"Linto and Laneer" takes its title from the opening poem, which is written in the Spenserian metre. It contains some good sentiments, and proves that the author is a keen lover of nature. The poem entitled "Hast thou Gold and Silver" is eminently suggestive. I am sorry that space does not permit my making quotations from such poems as "Old Jasper's Eagle," "England's Curse," "The Lame Teacher," "Hast thou Bread and Water," "When a Body's Humble," "Lend a Helping Hand," and several others of equal merit. But I think I have quoted sufficient to satisfy the reader that John Harris is a true poet and a sweet singer. In 1877, the late Lord Beaconsfield gave him a Government grant as a recognition of his literary industry and ability. His volumes are illustrated by the author's invalid son.

DE MONTFORT.

Works by John Harris.

Just published, elegantly and strongly bound in Cloth, with gilt back and side, illustrated by the Author's son, price 4s.

LINTO AND LANEER.

From THE CORNISHMAN, *December*, 1881.

More elegant in appearance than either of his numerous offspring. Many of the poems have the Excelsiorie, or true American ring. For simple beauty and naturalness they rank with the efforts of any of our modern bards. But best of all they are perfumed with the teachings of the Man of Calvary. The sacred poems at the end of the volume are not only original, but as graphic and beautiful as any of the poems on the same subject in the "Divine Tragedy" of Longfellow. One might as well attempt to critisize the thrilling notes of the lark as the wild flowers and diamonds in "Wayside Pictures," and "Linto and Laneer." The drawing-room tables and libraries in the cosy and stately homes of Cornwall are not what they should be without them.

From the WEST BRITON, *January*, 1882.

Were I to enumerate the pieces in the work deserving praise, my critique would extend to an almost indefinite length; so I must content myself by referring to a limited number of effusions which have in a peculiar sense won my admiration. "The Faces at the Pane" I consider as sweet and touching a lyric on the domestic affections as ever it has been my delight to read. It graphically portrays the strong and ardent love which exists between children and parents, breathing a spirit of sympathy and beauty. "Robert Burns" is a most worthy tribute to the worth and memory of that great minstrel. "The Test of Friendship" is written with a vigour and force which leaves an abiding impression upon the mind. "Our Feathered Teachers" is a beautiful lyric, melodious as the warblings of Nature's choir who fill the vales and woodlands with their flood of song. How well it speaks for the happy birds teaching man a lesson of gratitude and cheerfulness? "A Stainless Name" is worthy of Burns, and forcibly reminds me of the style of that mighty bard. I can well imagine that he would have sung of the same subject in a similar strain. I strongly recommend it to all who love and admire genuine poetry.
J. B. C.

From the CORNISH TELEGRAPH, *December*, 1881.

In his fifteenth publication the Cornish Poet comes before his readers. The press have been unanimous in their verdict on the originality, simplicity, and power of his poems. In his sixty-first year the author's fire and force remain unabated—perhaps they might be said to be in their fullest vigour. His power as a poet is perfect. He not only appeals to one's discrimination as a mere versifier, but there is a ring of honest manliness throughout the book. To those desirous of sending a present to friends abroad, none could be more acceptable than the last production of the Cornish Poet.

Testimony of George Smith, F.S.A., of Coalville, "The Children's Friend," August 30th, 1882.

"Thank you right heartily for 'Linto and Laneer.' It will do much good, and add lustre to your name upon earth while you are engaged in singing heavenly songs on the other side of the river."

HAMILTON, ADAMS AND CO.: LONDON.
THE AUTHOR: FALMOUTH.   JOHN GILL AND SON: PENRYN.

Strongly bound in cloth, Crown Quarto, with a PORTRAIT of the AUTHOR, price 12/6, the writer's COLLECTED WORKS, entitled

Wayside Pictures, Hymns & Poems.

These poems contain the true poetic ring. There is much in them to admire and ponder over. One hundred Hymns full of pure Gospel truth. John Harris has turned many gems of Scripture into verse, and we claim for him no small place among hymn-writers.—The *Literary World*.

Mr. Harris narrates many adventures in which the highest qualities are evinced.—The *London Figaro*.

LONDON: HAMILTON, ADAMS AND CO.
FALMOUTH: THE AUTHOR.   PENRYN: J. GILL AND SON.

Cloth superb, illustrated by the Author's son.   Price 3s. 6d.

TALES AND POEMS.

There is a homely simplicity in the Tales, and a true-hearted sympathy with nature and man in the Poems.—The *Literary World*.

The Tales are all marked by originality, and interest the reader to the end. The Poems are characterised by sweetness, pathos, and often a strange and unexpected power, and are sure to be popular.—*Brief*.

Tales and Poems is one of the most attractive books we have read for some time.—The *Hull Miscellany*.

LONDON: HAMILTON, ADAMS AND CO.
FALMOUTH: THE AUTHOR.   PENRYN: J. GILL & SON.

From the ATHENAEUM, *from 1856 to 1868.*

"Of John Harris we have ere this had pleasure in writing with praise as a simple natural poet, such as every race but too rarely produces, and of a kind which differs to the core from that of the sentimental and whining bards who so frequently publish what should be hidden. John Harris has earned a place by the side of Robert Bloomfield. He was a Cornish Miner, a hard worker who found food for fine fancies in the very bowels of the earth. He writes well. What we admire in his poetry is its simplicity, its honest piety, and the limitation of its matter to the facts of his own experience. Mr. Harris has written verses which, compared with those that spring from some ardent claimants on the public purse, are as the wine of flowers to the stagnant water of a froggy pool. His writing to any other age would have been a marvel, and it is a phenomenon even in our own—earnest, strong, and sweet with a father's love and all domestic affections. We testify fully to the freshness, vigour, and beauty of most of his verses. Mr. Harris fully deserves the approval of all those lovers of self-taught talent who may subscribe to or buy his books."

From the CRITIC.

We may safely say that the public have been educated in a high poetic school. Longfellow and Mackay are in spirit daily visiting our cottages; and these, even more than Shelley, Byron, and Scott, keep fresh and warm the popular taste for poetry. It becomes, then our duty to see that no wretched verses are foisted on the public with the dangerous plea that they are the performance of a peasant or an artisan. We must be careful that taste is not lowered. Therefore, not because Mr. Harris is a miner, but because he has the true instincts and perfect skill of the artist, we welcome his poems. No man can read these poems without feeling that at least one luminous or gifted man dignifies daily toil in the darkness of the mine. No man can read these poems without rising from their perusal a better man. A beautiful contentment shines from every page. Would that every King were like this man! We are loth to part from these poems which are so homely and so ennobling; but we have done good service, less perhaps to the author than to mankind, if we have helped the sale of them.